THAT WE MAY HAVE HOPE

*"For whatever things have been written
have been written for our instruction, that
through the patience and the consolation
afforded by the Scriptures, we may have
hope."*

ROMANS, 15:4

THAT

WE MAY HAVE
HOPE

Reflections on the Epistles

for the Sunday Masses and

some of the feasts

by WILLIAM A. DONAGHY, S.J.

Author of "Hear Ye Him"

THE AMERICA PRESS, NEW YORK

Imprimi Potest:
    William E. FitzGerald, S.J.
        Provincial: New England Province

Nihil Obstat:
    Rt. Rev. Msgr. John M. A. Fearns, S.T.D.
    Censor Librorum

Imprimatur:
    ✠ Francis Cardinal Spellman, D.D.
    Archbishop of New York

                    March 18, 1954

60

To my Godparents
Col. James K. Donaghy
Mrs. Barbara Donaghy Quinn

CONTENTS

Contents

FOREWORD

This volume will swell the number of books recently written about the Scriptures without, in any distinguished way, being a notable addition. Its purpose is simple and humble. The author knows from professional experience as a retreat master that the faithful are easily discouraged by the difficulties of Holy Writ and too ready to relinquish it to scholars and exegetes. This is an attempt to induce such timid souls once more to open the holy books and find in them the kind of riches which one never acquires without mining. These reflections presuppose that one has read the Epistle of the Sunday or has it by him. I am very grateful to my former confreres on *America* for permission to reprint columns originally published in the department, *The Word*, as well as other essays which, at various times, appeared in their pages.

WILLIAM A. DONAGHY, S.J.,
Campion Hall
Jesuit Retreat House
North Andover, Mass.

THAT WE MAY HAVE HOPE

With Fitting Honor Prepare

The Communion Prayer

There are two Advents now, two seasons of preparation for the festival of Christ's birth—the Christian and the commercial. And it is a stinging reproach to us that the predicates which should primarily pertain to the Christian Advent—seriousness, zeal, thoroughness—better describe the commercial. Advertising men sprain superlatives and have language leaking at the seams in their attempt to describe the goods in their stores; window-dressers wring ingenuity dry to make their displays attractive and arresting; special details of police channel crowds on their mercantile pilgrimage; newspapers caution us of the tidal flow of shopping days.

There is small danger that people will forget Christmas;

there is real danger that they may forget Christ. The thousands transfixed before the glittering stores may be oblivious of the telling tableau in the stable; the crowds pushing and struggling at the bargain counters—sometimes in a spirit anything but seasonal—may be as unaware of the central fact of Christmas as were those who, centuries ago, thronged for the census-taking into the city of David. People who anxiously check their lists lest they overlook and offend a friend destined for a gift or greeting card, can be totally blind to the central contradiction that He whose birthday it is has no place on their lists or in their hearts. Christmas can become and has become for many a merely social and humanitarian celebration, deriving rather from Dickens than from Saint Luke.

The Advent liturgy, though, is alive with the spirit of alert preparedness. Saint Paul, in the epistle for the first Sunday, summons us to shake off spiritual sloth, to wake from sleep, to put off the works of darkness and be vigilant to greet the day. The gospel shakes with the roar of toppling cities and the revelation of the second coming of the Son of Man—then no lovely Child and Redeemer, but the Divine Judge of the living and dead. In the Communion prayer of the Holy Sacrifice, we beg grace "that we may with fitting honor prepare for the approaching solemnities of our redemption."

Advent is no period of supine waiting but a time of energetic work. Paul, whose brilliant, dogmatic letters always introduce practical conclusions and suggestions for reducing dogma to everyday deed, exhorts the Romans and us "to put on the armor of light." Spiritual hypocrisy, self-deception, Pharisaism, insincerity, duplicity—these must be eradicated. "Let us walk honestly, as in the day"; not furtively, with the mind and soul darkened, but as children and lovers of the light.

He further specifies sins to be avoided—and the warning applies to the modern American as well as to the ancient Roman—revelry, bawdiness and impurity of all kinds, fractiousness and envy. The endeavor of Advent therefore is to make the human heart like the stable of Bethlehem, humble, unostentatious, unsullied by worldliness—in the hope that if the heart be like the stable, Christ may be, this Christmas morn, reborn in it.

Saint Augustine, in the seventh book of his *Confessions,* tells us that it was this passage from Romans, read in the Holy Sacrifice on the first Sunday of Advent, which was the occasion of his conversion. Opening the epistle, he read "not in rioting and drunkenness, not in chamberings and impurities, not in contentions and envy; but put ye on the Lord Jesus Christ and make not provision for the flesh in its concupiscences." "I did not wish to read," writes Augustine, "I did not read any further, for at the end of this sentence, immediately, as if the light of certainty had been poured into my heart, all the darkness of doubt was dispelled." May the sword-thrust of a similar grace strike into our hearts this first Sunday of Advent, and arouse us to imitate in good part Augustine's generosity with God.

That We May Have Hope

Romans 15:4

Some of the Fathers of the Church had the beautiful custom of referring to the Scriptures as letters from the Heavenly Father to us, His children, who are still exiles and wayfarers. In the dawn of the world, says Saint John Chrysostom, God walked familiarly with man, communicated directly with him: but man cut himself off, became unworthy of that high intimacy and, after that, God dealt with him aloofly, through the words of prophets and hagiographers. From that distant city to which we bend our steps, Saint Augustine writes, come letters to us, the pages of Holy Writ.

Now this is no mere pious fancy, but one mode of expressing a profound truth. For the fact of the matter is that

God is the primary and the principal author of Scripture, while the prophet or evangelist is the secondary and instrumental co-author. So we find Saint Paul, in the epistle for the second Sunday in Advent, assuring us, "whatever things have been written, have been written for our instruction, that through the patience and the consolation afforded by the Scriptures we may have hope."

In a great letter on the study and reading of Scripture, Pope Benedict XV quotes that phrase, "consolation afforded by the Scriptures," and praises the saintly and learned men who, in every age, have arisen to open up by their zeal and scholarship the treasures of the Bible to the people. One of the commonest calumnies against the Church is that she discourages the reading of the Bible. She is, of course, maternally alert lest her children read loose or inaccurate versions; she superintends the sacred text with the reverence which God's words deserve; she admits that certain passages need explanation and encourages her scholars to clear up obscurities; she tries to defend us from the fatal attitude of private interpretation with all its contradictory consequences. But she has never ceased to hold out the sacred books to us as an inexhaustible treasure of instruction and solace. Benedict writes: "Hence, as far as in us lies, we . . . shall . . . never desist from urging the faithful to read daily the Gospels, the Acts and the Epistles, so as to gather thence food for their souls." Pope Pius X was of the same mind; Pope Leo XIII granted an indulgence to those who daily read the Scriptures for at least a quarter of an hour.

The trouble with the New Testament, said Chesterton, is that it is no longer *new*. We have come to take it for granted; we hear a fragment of it read in the Holy Sacrifice, but never attempt to explore it ourselves. Perhaps that is why we know so little about Christ—and little knowledge means little love. "Ignorance of the Bible," wrote Saint Jerome, "means ignorance of Christ"—a judgment which Pope Benedict XV quoted approvingly. We all have the obligation of prayer and spiritual reading; Catholicism is not merely a matter of rushing around doing good, back and forth, to and fro, with the tireless energy, range, scope and depth of a windshield-wiper. Catholicism is a deep force within, to be increased by prayer and the knowledge of Christ.

Take your New Testament as though it were actually *new* to you. God is all around you like a sea if you are in the state of grace. Advert consciously to His presence, ask Him for light to see the truth, strength to embrace it, for the grace you personally need. Then open and read. This is God's letter to you and it well might be called a love-letter since its every page records His love for you. Read it as you would a love-letter, slowly, savoring every phrase, searching for every nuance, seeking each implication.

Specifically now in Advent, how could one better employ himself than in reading Saint Luke's first two chapters, derived from Our Lady, whom Saint Jerome called "the library of the apostles"? The Middle Ages termed those chapters "the golden gospel" and they can immeasurably enrich your soul, enlarge your heart.

Rejoice in the Lord

Philippians 4:4

The Macedonian city of Philippi, elevated by the Emperor Augustus to the dignity of a Roman colony, was peopled by great ghosts, alive with the whisperings of history. Philip filled his coffers with the gold of the region; the surrounding marshes had rung with the battles between Brutus and Octavius, Antony and Cassius, and had heard Brutus' sad lament, which Shakespeare formulates: "here in Philippi fields, I know my hour is come." Most important of all, it was at Philippi that Christianity secured its first beachhead on the European continent. The church which Saint Paul founded there was the dearest of his communities, his "joy and . . . crown" (Phil. 4:1) and the Philippians returned his affection multiplied, sending him generous alms (Phil. 4:15) on which he subsisted while he was in Corinth (2 Cor. 11:9).

We can imagine their grief, then, when news ran along the Mediterranean coast that Paul, in custody of the Centurion Julius, was under arrest and on his way to Rome. Immediately the Philippians dispatched Epaphroditus to find how it fared with the apostle. This courageous messenger stayed with Paul, assisted him in his fettered ministry, as "my brother and fellow-laborer" (Phil. 2:25), had a nearly fatal illness, and then returned to Philippi bearing a letter from Paul. The epistle is a passionate outpouring of his love for his distant brethren, alight with recurrent and paradoxical joy; and a section of it is read in the Holy Sacrifice for Gaudete Sunday, the third of Advent.

The first chapter burns with his apostolic charity toward them: in the second, he exhorts them to unity, to an imitation of the Christ who humbled Himself even unto death, and to holy fear and trembling in the quest for salvation. Their faith is their glory and so "you also rejoice in the Lord," and he subjoins his perennial warning against false teachers. The fourth chapter returns to the irrepressible theme of joy, and here occurs the passage read in this Sunday's Mass: "Rejoice in the Lord always: again, I say, rejoice," a message which the concluding lines of the missive reiterate: "Now I rejoice in the Lord exceedingly" (4:10).

The point is inescapable and important. "Today," writes Agnes Repplier, "we make scant pretense of cheerfulness: and absurdities, when recognized, seem insurmountable to some and inspirational to others. Strange coercive drives pursue us relentlessly and leave us drained of purpose." It recalls Matthew Arnold's somber summary: "For most men in a brazen prison live"; and for them, this Pauline call to joy, written from an actual prison, has real significance. We like to think of ourselves as a happy people: our local Broadways are ablaze with temples dedicated to a good time; we spend millions on merriment; entertainment is a booming business. But behind and below our laughter is the scarcely submerged catch of hysteria, the swelling sob of fear. Genuine joy is not a matter of the quaffed cocktail or the smart sally which sets "the table in a roar"; it is an attitude, an atmosphere of the mind not subject to the moody meteorology of the outer world.

Notice that Saint Paul does not say simply "Rejoice," but *"rejoice in the Lord,"* thereby rooting and anchoring happiness in Him who is unchangeable, "yesterday, and to-day: and the same forever" (Heb. 13:8). It is the realization that we live *in Christ* that fixes our serenity high above the ebb and flow of transient whim, capricious feelings. "Whether we live, we live unto the Lord" (Rom. 14:7-8); "though we have nothing, yet we possess all things" (2 Cor. 6:10), and life for us is a "glory in the Lord" (1 Cor. 1:31).

Christmas is a day on which we renew these realizations and rejoice in them, as we look on the tiny Christ, cradled in the arms of His Virgin Mother. He is our joy, our hope, our assurance: and there is rich theological significance in that title of Our Lady which salutes her as "the Cause of our Joy."

Everyone Will Have His Praise from God

I Corinthians 4:5

Rafael, Cardinal Merry Del Val, brilliant diplomat, ecclesiastic and Papal Secretary of State, whose greatest glory was the secret saintliness of his private life, once characterized Christmas as "a feast of joyous abasement." It is a packed phrase, reminding us once again of God's infinite love, which impelled Him to send His only-begotten Son to save us; of the generosity and joy with which the Word of God "emptied Himself, taking the form of a servant, being made in the likeness of men" (Phil. 2:7). Likewise it indicates the sentiment we should feel in our own souls. Unless you become as little children, you cannot appreciate the message of Bethlehem, where God became a little Child. The proud, the cynical, the worldly, the sophisticated find the stable cold and not a little boring.

But if one sincerely tries to reproduce in one's heart some of the humility which Bethlehem so compellingly holds up to us, he will not be an awkward stranger in the presence of Jesus, Mary and Joseph. "Self-abasement," the Cardinal continues, "is a wonderful source of union with God, provided it is sincere; and, if it be joyful and childlike, there is no discouragement or despondency in it."

What a difference this birth in Bethlehem would make in every human life. There was a humble town down on the lake shore, that night when Christ was born, engulfed in darkness. It had no claim on fame, no title to remembrance; it should have been erased by the sandstorms and swept into oblivion. Yet it is forever exalted, immortalized in the surname of its most distinguished citizen; it will be recalled as long as men speak. The town was Magdala; Mary Magdalen came from there. Perhaps her mother stood that night looking down on her child, asleep with the bright halo of hair on her pillow, and mused about her daughter's future. She might be a great lady in Israel! But she became a sinner and, humbling herself in penitence, was exalted to sainthood through the infinite mercy of Jesus Christ.

There was another tiny town in Palestine that night which had no lease on history either. It was unimportant, inconsequential. Yet it will be forever infamous because of one of its citizens. The town was Kerioth: Judas Iscariot came from there. He was called to be a saint, but he exalted himself and fell from the eminence of self-esteem, perhaps into eternal perdition. Out on the lake that night was a young fisherman, brawny and tanned; how could he have known that he would become the first in the dynasty which

Macaulay so rapturously hailed; how could he have suspected that the ring of the fisherman would become one of the central symbols of Western civilization, that Peter would be a name famous in time and eternity?

What a difference this birth made in every human life. It made a difference in yours, too: but has it made enough of a difference? Look into your heart for the answer.

In his *Book of Miracles*, Saint Gregory of Tours has a charming story, suited by its simplicity to the season. There is a well, he says, at Bethlehem, where Our Lady drew water; and if the faithful gather around it, a linen cloth over their heads, "to such as are clean of heart, the same star appears that was seen by the Magi." Many may look; but only the worthy see.

Deep as a well is the human heart; and if you look into your own, with the cloth signifying that recollection which shuts out the glamour and clamor of the world over your head, you may see in the deeps the star which only the worthy behold, the star that leads to Jesus and Mary.

The Fullness of Time

Galatians 4:4

Hilaire Belloc, writing on artistic inspiration, mentions one source of it which our blasé day might well overlook. Contemplating a statue, he muses: "what a good thing it would be if men were to return for inspiration to innocence"—which, he adds, has something far more substantial and solid than either the frenzied search for the new or involved invention. Many of the works which lift the human heart in a Wordsworthian leap of exultance, he declares, "have the particular quality of youth—I mean of very early youth." Even George Moore, surprisingly enough, found modern painting dull and savorless because it had no "innocency" in it.

These thoughts, obviously, are suggested by Bethlehem, which is at once inexhaustibly inspirational and an immortal monument to innocence. Any mother and any child, in their mutual relationship of brooding love and helpless dependence, will induce in the hardened cynic a fleeting nostalgia for the days of his youth, the days of his innocence. But this virginal mother—spotless, sinless, radiant—and her small Son, the divine Redeemer, constitute an ultimate challenge to any mind intelligent enough to apprehend the terms of the proposition that God became man in order that man might become God.

Bethlehem is so blunt, so unequivocal, so embarrassingly clear in its implications, that no one can rest secure in his possession of a code of worldly principles there. Christ as the author of human life is also the supreme authority on it; and before the manger which encompasses Him whom the heavens cannot contain, one is bound to ask: What really matters? What basically is important? What, in the wintry light of this cattle shed, is the real perspective on such evasive and shifting notions as success, true wealth, genuine achievement?

The eternal Word of God might have become man in any fashion He desired. He could have come in rolling thunders and confluent lightnings, in a reversal of Elias' fiery chariot, with ten million bugles braying and all creation fixed at attention in one reverberant "alleluia." But the script of Christ's birth was written not in Hollywood but Heaven; He deliberately elected to come so quietly, so undistinguishedly, that very few people knew about it. The first who came to adore Him were shepherds and that, too, was richly significant. For in the old days of the patriarchs, the keeping of sheep had been the honorable occupation of Abraham, Isaac, Jacob and David; but it had fallen on bad times. At the time of Our Lord's birth, the nomadic, desert shepherds were a despised group. They lived far from the Temple, ignorant of the legal observances which the Pharisees accounted essential to salvation. They were suspected of thievery, put on a level with publicans, and their testimony was not acceptable in court.

It was most fitting, then, that the God who was born for the sick and the sinner, the underprivileged and the unknown, should have had as His first witnesses those who would most benefit by His coming. He came to delight and encourage those who had retained their innocence, to deliver and sustain those who had lost theirs; innocence as inspiration produced its masterpiece at Bethlehem.

Kneel there in meditation during this Christmas octave and be inspired to greater faith, unshakable hope, profound love. Christ has made it easy for you to approach Him; there is no protocol, no ceremony; the accent is on accessibility. In the Office of Saint Martin of Tours occurs the beautiful sentiment: "Our Lord Jesus Christ said not that He would come clad in purple or adorned with a crown." As an adult He would tell the inquiring multitudes that such "are in the houses of kings" (Matt. 11:8) and He would refuse their crown (John 6:15). From them and from us He wants only love. Looking at the small King of Heaven and His Queen, clad in that candent innocence whose reflected light shows us the deviousness and darkness of our own souls, we should arise strongly determined to be more like Him who, by His birth, as Saint Paul tells us, became our brother.

In the Name of the Lord Jesus Christ

Acts 4:10

Jerusalem was in a ferment. Jesus of Nazareth was dead, but hardly had His enemies embalmed His memory in obloquy when the rumor ran around the town that He had risen. In the next few weeks, rumor ripened into conviction: and then, spiraling out of the heavens, came a vortex of wind to focus on a house which sheltered His mother and His disciples. These latter, suddenly articulate and authoritatively eloquent, began to preach His messiahship, His resurrection and divinity, making many converts who pooled their possessions in communal charity and worshiped each day in the Temple and in their homes. "Fear came upon every soul"; nor could the wrath or the sarcasm of the chief priests stem the flooding enthusiasm; "for many wonders also and signs were done by means of the apostles in Jerusalem."

In these dramatic circumstances, Peter and John entered the Temple one afternoon, and were halted by the piteous cry of a twisted paralytic near one of the gates. Peter told the cripple he could not give alms: "Silver and gold I have none; but what I have, that I give thee. In the name of Jesus Christ of Nazareth, arise and walk" (Acts 3:6). Strength surged through shriveled sinew and withered muscle, the man leapt up and, in a transport of thanks, "clung to Peter and John," while the first Pontiff took occasion to preach to the curious bystanders on Him in whose name the miracle occurred.

Within the Temple precincts they were under jurisdiction of the priests, who at once arrested the apostles. After a night in custody, they stood before the Council, and the glowering faces of Annas and Caiphas must have jogged their memories. "By what authority or in what name have you done this?" The judicial question rang through the hall; and Peter who had run away one night, Peter who had warmed his hands and denied his Lord, now filled with the Holy Spirit, replied at length: "Be it known to all of you and to all the people of Israel that in the name of Jesus Christ of Nazareth, whom you crucified, whom God has raised from the dead, even in this name, does he (the cripple) stand here before you, sound" (Acts 4:1-13). Confounded by the courage of Peter, the simplicity of his position and the cogency of his evidence, the Council lamely enjoined silence on him and his companions, though Peter protested that they were under the apostolic necessity to "speak of what we have seen and heard." This whole moving scene is revived for us by the epistle for the Feast of the Holy Name of Jesus—which is a section of Peter's response to the Council.

His invocation of the Holy Name is, in fact, a swift summary of the faith, as Peter himself pointed out: "Neither is there salvation in any other. For there is no other name under heaven given to men by which we must be saved." "What, think you, has made the light of faith to shine so brightly and so suddenly in the whole world, but the preaching of the name of Jesus?" asks Saint Bernard. This is the name, he adds, which Paul "was bidden to carry before kings, and Gentiles, and the children of Israel, and he carried that name as a light."

So it would always be. That sacred name would gleam on the white banner of Joan of Arc; it would be whispered by saints like Blessed Margaret Clitherow, wife, mother and martyr, described by Sigrid Undset, horribly crushed to death for His sake with His name on her lips; or by Blessed Robert Southwell, poet and priest, one of England's most exquisite spirits, tortured diabolically by Topcliffe, afterwards hanged, drawn and quartered with the sacred name in mouth and heart.

So it must be with us. That name above all names (Phil. 2:9), so often voiced by blasphemous men as an expletive, should be for us the briefest and dearest of ejaculations. Meaning, as it does, "saviour," it should be a banner to us, a balm and a bandage, a hope and an assurance, a sweet memory, as Bernard says, in life and death—and happiness forever.

A Heart of Mercy . . . Humility . . . Patience

Colossians 3:12

Two of the concepts exalted and canonized by the first Christmas were the ideas of motherhood and childhood. After Bethlehem, woman was no longer, in the quietly barbarous phrase of a pagan poet, "the recreation of the warrior"; nor was the child any more a defenseless chattel dependent for his right to live on the whim of his father. There are, to be sure, large, loquacious groups even yet who would transfer the principles of selective breeding from the farm to the family; there are many who espouse the Shavian position that the genetic process which produces Holsteins would, if applied to the human field, result in Einsteins. But right-thinking men still regard motherhood as a sacred institution; they still look on the child as holy. To such, the feast of the Holy Family, falling on the Sunday within the octave of Epiphany, must always be a precious day.

The shepherds have departed and the wise men: there for our veneration and meditation are the holy three—Joseph, model of fathers, model of men; Mary, inspiration of women; and Jesus Christ, the light of the world. Here is the first Christian family, and the best, the pattern to which all families must conform. It is a pattern easy to perceive and understand, but difficult to live by while human beings remain selfish. The father is the head of the family, the law of it and the logic; the mother is the heart, the sweetness and the love.

But authors and painters have dilated sufficiently on the glory of real motherhood. It is not altogether an abrupt transition to turn for a moment to another, vicarious, motherhood which continues the virgin maternalism of Our Lady. The Christmas season, with its emphasis on virginity and motherhood, might well remind us of those who, in their humility, prefer the neglect which is too often their lot—our nuns. They are "the women who . . . followed Him" (Luke 23:49), "the virgins . . . who follow the Lamb wherever He goes" (Apoc. 14:4). They can say with Saint Agnes, in the liturgy: "He has put a seal on my countenance, so that I have no lover besides Him"; they are the sisters of Saint Cecilia of whom the Breviary says: "The glorious virgin always carried the gospel of Christ in her breast." Consecrating the possibility of natural motherhood, they dedicate themselves to the supernatural motherhood of caring for Christ's little ones, be they children in the schools, the sick in hospitals or the aged battered by sharp winds in the twilight of life. No one has a better right to be at Bethlehem than a nun. Perhaps no one has a better appreciation of Bethlehem than she who is by instinct a mother, by grace a virgin.

Yet nuns are often the object of misunderstanding, even from Catholics, who overlook their excellences, exaggerate their imperfections, minimize their sacrifices. Frances Parkinson Keyes, in her *Written in Heaven,* comes much closer to the truth when she pens a glowing tribute to their sanity, sanctity, intelligence and general outlook. So does that redoubtable, highly cultivated Yankee lady, Mary Ellen Chase, in *This Goodly Fellowship,* which tells us how, from living with nuns, she came to love them.

Day in and day out, in the Bethlehems and Nazareths which are their convents, they call down God's blessings on the world. It is a reminder to us of the pervasive power of prayer, that the apostolic patron of the foreign missions, after the great Xavier, is a Carmelite nun who lived her brief, beautiful life in a convent in France—the Little Flower of Jesus. It is likewise a reminder to us of the influence nuns exert on this sad earth. Monsignor Dupanloup once suggested an advertisement in the papers asking for thousands of women to turn their backs on their prospects and to devote themselves to lives of patient perseverance and hard work out of love. What a quixotic request! Yet there are such women in the world, living perpetuations of Mary, thousands and thousands of them, in our convents.

Let Love Be without Pretense

Romans 12:9

While it is a compelling and justly famous sales-phrase for a company dealing in paints, the slogan "save the surface and you save all" is an extremely vicious principle in the spiritual life. It is the fundamental axiom of that Pharisaism, ancient and modern, which accentuates appearance at the expense of genuineness, substituting for rooted holiness a superficial respectability, cutting down Christianity to its own little code.

Our holy faith represents not merely the skittering waves of surface activity but more essentially those deeps which are quiet, contemplative, alive with the indwelling God. So Saint Paul constantly insisted, and he repeats the assertion in that section of Romans read as the epistle in the Mass for the second Sunday after Epiphany. "Let love," he tells us, "be without pretense"; and, in a series of brief, jolting admonitions, goes on to indicate that deeper, inner Catholicism which, if neglected and unprotected, can rust away within any of us.

Many there are who from habit and a sense of fitness would never miss Mass on Sunday. But their attendance at the Holy Sacrifice is rather that of physical presence than spiritual participation. They have no real appreciation of the incredible drama which unfolds before them, though for years they have dedicated weekly an unintelligent and impatient half-hour to it. The frequent reception of Holy Communion, involving previous confession and the Eucharistic fast, seems to them too much for Christ to expect.

They are not saints, they tell you, but good Catholics none the less—better than many another. They find it not at all irreconcilable with their religion to indulge in sharp business practice. Deviousness, lying, misrepresentation are legitimate devices in commerce where greed is the only creed. So they fall into that quiet secularism which holds that the faith, if it overflows from Sunday into the weekdays, out of the Church into the office, means failure. They make a Bible of a bankbook, and solvency a sacrament.

One may suspect that such people seldom read or listen to Saint Paul. But even if they did, the exhortation in today's epistle: "Love one another with fraternal charity, anticipating one another with honor," would seem to them downright naive. They would still feel free to reveal even the serious faults of another; they relish a particularly ugly item of gossip as a gourmet rolls a fine old wine on his tongue; the hunting season on human reputations is always open and hampered by no limitations either of time or type of weapon. They are historically aware of Christ's central law of charity, but that knowledge seldom seeps down into the order of present action. Not only individuals feel their contempt, but even whole races who because of birth, background or color are repugnant to these insular little minds.

A far cry indeed from them is the Christian whom Paul reveals by implication in the epistle of this week: "Be not slothful . . . be fervent . . . serving the Lord . . . be patient in tribulation . . . persevering in prayer. Bless those who persecute you; bless and do not curse. . . . Be of one mind towards one another."

It is difficult if not impossible to read Saint Paul and go on deceiving oneself. Read today's epistle, for example, and hold it up as a mirror before your own soul. How deep, how genuine is your Catholicism? Is it merely a limited set of carefully selected external forms and fulfillments, or is it actually the full acceptance of all those interior convictions deriving from dogma and depending on grace which exteriorize themselves in a real Catholic life? Are you saving your surface or saving your soul?

But One Receives a Prize

I Corinthians 9:24

In the tight, dramatic economy of the liturgical year, the life of Our Lord is contracted to skeletal outline. With Christmas still a green memory, therefore, and the New Year scarcely out of swaddling clothes, we find Septuagesima Sunday upon us. Christmas is a feast of sweetness, of childhood, of consolation. The Circumcision and the conferring of the Sacred Name on Our Lord is a day of joy. Epiphany is the happy anniversary of the revelation of the King to the Gentiles.

But Septuagesima and the season it inaugurates are a reminder to us of the harsher realities of the faith. For the ultimate climax of Bethlehem is Calvary; it was on Calvary that the name "Jesus," the Saviour, was translated into blood and sweat and salvation; the Child visited by a few wondering Magi on Epiphany is revealed to the ages in full stature on Calvary, being lifted up that He might draw all men to Himself. Calvary is the termination of the liturgical cycle ushered in by Septuagesima. In order that we may approach that holy hill with proper reverence and appreciation, the Church calls on us to go through a long period of preparation, of spiritual "training," so to speak, a figure which Saint Paul employs in the Septuagesima epistle.

In ancient days, periodic athletic contests engaged the minds and muscles of the competitive young. Such were the Olympian and Isthmian games, and to achieve victory in these was a motive which nerved the athletes of the time to endure a "training" regimen of cruel austerity. Epictetus and the unathletic Horace have left us famous descriptions of the sufferings, sweatings, shiverings and general self-repression which the contenders underwent to condition themselves for these games. The Isthmian games were held at Corinth, and Saint Paul, writing to the Corinthians in the section which is read in the Septuagesima Mass, draws his sinewy imagery from that familiar fact.

"Do you not know," he asks, "that those who run in a race, all indeed run, but one receives the prize? So run as to obtain it. And everyone in a contest abstains from all things—and they indeed to receive a perishable crown, but we an imperishable." The reasoning is perfectly clear. An athlete is more zealous for the applause of the multitude than we are for the approval of God; he hammers his body into hardness, through brutal training, to win a garland that wilts within the day, while we begrudge, when we cannot evade, those sacrifices which could bring us unwithering beatitude.

There is no safe, easy short cut to heaven; it is a contest, a battle—not a pointless feverishness but a purposive, determined drive. "I, therefore," says Paul, "so run as not without a purpose; I fight as not beating the air; but I chastise my body and bring it into subjection, lest perhaps after preaching to others I myself should be rejected." So often we miss the multitudinous opportunities which life provides us for mortification and self-discipline. We suffer—a headache, a slight, an insult—but instead of sanctifying our pain by proper motive, we rebel against it, waste our spiritual substance in fruitless wailing. We run, but "without a purpose." So often the difficulties of life buffet us and we lash back blindly at what we stupidly call chance, luck or fate: we fight, indeed, but "as beating the air."

In the concluding paragraph of the section, Paul recalls the spiritual glories of the chosen people. Yet, despite the divine munificence, they turned from God—"with most of them God was not well pleased." What of you individually? What use have you made of the largess God has showered on you? Have you a Pauline virility of spirit or is your spiritual life "without a purpose," a matter of "beating the air"? Is God well pleased with you? These are some of the questions which Septuagesima poses to us as it opens a period of penance and preparation during which we should reappraise and, if necessary, reorganize our spiritual lives.

My Grace Is Sufficient

2 Corinthians 12:9

Saint John Chrysostom, in one of his several tributes to Saint Paul, declared, that the heart of this great apostle "might be called without error the heart of the whole world . . . That heart was so expansive as to receive within it whole cities, peoples and nations." In those words he merely developed the compact epigram *Cor Pauli, Cor Christi—* the heart of Paul was the heart of Christ.

Sexagesima Sunday particularly honors the apostle. Through the epistle of the Mass, longest of the year, one can feel the seismic heartbeat of Christ's indefatigable envoy.

In dissolute Corinth, Paul, by zealous prayer and work, had established a Christian nucleus. All around his little flock swirled the full foulness of paganism, and he continually worried lest his neophytes be inoculated with worldliness. Titus, his disciple, reporting from the field, confirmed his worst fears and occasioned his second letter to Corinth, a letter which is intensely personal and passionately sincere.

False prophets and pseudo-apostles had confused the Christian Corinthians and split them into quarreling factions. They had impugned Paul's apostolate, undermined his authority, jeered at his unprepossessing person (2 Cor. 10:10). This section of his letter is a review of his credentials, a defense of his life and teaching.

He is a Hebrew, he tells them, an Israelite, a minister of Christ, and more—an apostle. On his broken body he carried the scars of his love for Jesus Christ. Scourgings, stoning, shipwreck, labor, hardship, hunger, thirst, cold, nakedness, betrayals and the constant agony of anxiety lest his converts fall away again, had wounded his body and his soul. Not only had he suffered for Christ; he had received great favors from Him; and he passes from a catalog of his crosses to give them a glimpse of the mystical heights to which God had elevated him.

It is a thrilling revelation of Paul's love for his Lord, which throws into humiliating contrast our own petty devotion and limited service. It is an *apologia*, but despite the prominence of the personal pronoun, it is primarily a hymn of humility. For all of these sufferings were endured, all these glories enjoyed, through the power of God. As for Paul himself: "If I must boast, I will boast of the things that concern my weakness"; and again, "I will glory in nothing save in my infirmities." Even after these human vexations and divine visitations, Paul was still tormented by some persistent illness. But when he begged God for relief, the answer came: "My grace is sufficient for thee, for strength is made perfect in weakness."

Christ Himself had told us: "when you have done everything that was commanded you, say: 'We are unprofitable servants; we have done what it was our duty to do'" (Luke 17:10). Hence Paul, the tireless herald of Christ, was not exalted either by the labors he sustained or the favors he received, but humbly acknowledged: "For when I am weak, then am I strong."

If that was his reaction to his heroic ministries, what should our reflections be, since we are so far from "doing everything that was commanded." The prayer of the Sexagesima Mass puts words into our mouths that should induce an attitude in our minds: "O God, who seest that we put not our trust in anything that we do of ourselves; mercifully grant that by the protection of the Apostle of the Gentiles, we may be defended against all adversities."

But to make that prayer intelligently and sincerely, we must be certain that we have not fallen into the heresy of self-sufficiency or into spiritual pride or smugness of soul.

Made to Stumble

2 Corinthians 11:29

The Sexagesima epistle, longest of the year, is packed with tumultuous thought, afire with passionate eloquence. It is a section from Paul's second letter to Corinth, in which he justifies himself and his work at a time when some of the fickle Corinthians, seduced by false teachers, were wavering in their loyalty to him and the Christ he preached. Out of the letter there arises Paul the apostle, indomitable lover and defender of Christ, sick, wan with prison pallor, his breast and back laced by the scourges; pushing on through wilderness and mountain pass despite lurking bandits and prowling beasts; shipwrecked, betrayed, hungry, cold, thirsty—yet ever driven by the apostolic necessity of bringing Christ to men, men to Christ. And now news has come to him that some of his flock, lured by hireling shepherds, are looking towards speciously green meadows beyond the pale: and all the brilliance of his mind and blazing heart explodes in this letter.

In its compressed riches there is one small phrase, worthy of pondering, which we could easily overlook. Talking about the possible defection of some of his converts, he asks: "Who is made to stumble and I am not inflamed?" Now those words, "made to stumble," are extremely interesting; and, if we fully apprehend their meaning, we shall have an accurate idea of an important spiritual truth. In the Greek and Latin texts those three words are expressed in one verb; and the root, the core of that verb, in both languages, is "scandal" (*scandalizatur* and *skandalizetai*).

In Greek, the noun "scandal" originally meant a stick or trigger of a trap, on which the bait was placed, so that the trap would spring when an unwary animal nibbled at it. The verb form signifies to entrap, to set a trap or to cause to stumble. The Douay version translates this passage: "Who is scandalized, and I am not on fire?" Monsignor Knox renders it: "Is anyone's conscience hurt? I am ablaze with indignation." The Confraternity edition has the wording previously quoted: "Who is made to stumble and I am not inflamed?" All of these renditions have merit. They show us Paul, as the zealous pastor, concerned about the souls under him, identifying himself with their sorrows; but they likewise give us a fairly adequate concept of the foul sin that is scandal. According to Saint Thomas Aquinas, scandal consists in a word or action, evil in itself, which occasions the spiritual ruin of another. By it, the person giving scandal entraps another, as it were, entangles him in sin, causes him to stumble morally, hurts his conscience. And

Paul shared his Divine Master's indignation at such treachery. "Whoever causes one of these little ones who believe in me to sin," Christ said, "it were better for him to have a great millstone hung round his neck, and to be drowned in the depths of the sea. . . . Woe to the world because of scandals! For it must needs be that scandals come, but woe to the man through whom scandal does come!" (Matt. 18:6-8).

What, then, of those parents who by sins of profane speech, uncontrolled temper, failure to meet their religious obligations, give scandal to their own little ones who are also God's little ones? What of the Catholic-school graduate who repudiates his heritage, spurns his principles and lets expediency, greed or simple lust shape his life and beslime his soul? What of the average Catholic, with his divinely enjoined obligation of letting his light shine before men that their hearts and minds may be lifted to the heavenly Father, who, instead, in politics, in his profession, in business, in his writings, gives scandal, and encourages evil men to continue so and entices good men to desert their standards?

What about your own daily life? Is it a bright example or a constant scandal? Do people see a great cleavage between your Catholic profession and your daily performance? Are they confirmed in their own contempt of religion by your hypocrisy? "It is good . . ." Paul warned the Romans, "not to do anything by which thy brother is offended or scandalized or weakened" (Rom. 14:21).

Sounding Brass and a Tinkling Cymbal

I Corinthians 13:1

Erasmus' comparison of Saint Paul's style and thought to a river is singularly fortunate. For his words show all the moods of a stream; they darken when his overhanging mind is clouded with worry; they quiver and shine when his topic is joyous; they slide smoothly through deep canyons of thought or tumble foaming over abrupt drops; they glitter into rapids, flatten out into broad expanses, wander off into estuaries. His First Epistle to the Corinthians, perhaps the most famous of his letters, reprinted in part by M. Lincoln Schuster in his *The World's Great Letters,* illustrates all this; and the passage read in the Mass for Quinquagesima Sunday is Paul at his most characteristic.

Long before, the prophet Joel had foretold that the age

of the Messiah would be marked by an outpouring of the
Spirit, that the first converts would be gifted with miraculous powers (Joel 2:28), a prophecy to which Peter ap-
pealed in his Pentecostal sermon (Acts 2:16). These extraordinary endowments—prophecy, the power to speak
various tongues and to heal the sick—were divinely designed
as an external indication of the internal grace of conversion
and as a means of disseminating the Christian doctrine.
But so boundless is man's capacity for missing the point
and exalting himself, that these powers were regarded by
some of their possessors as personal; they became the occasion of self-glorification, of unseemly rivalry and envy. This
was the situation in the early Corinthian Church and
against it Paul lashes out, capping his rebuke with the
incredibly beautiful description of charity.

Charity is above all, charity must be in all, charity is the
queen of the virtues and it must rule all gifts and powers.
No matter what faculties a man may have, if he has not got
charity, they are all sound and fury signifying nothing. The
gift of tongues, prophecy, philanthropy—without charity
they are soulless shells.

This was Paul's central theme and fundamental thesis.
"Owe no man anything," he tells the Romans, "except to
love one another; for he who loves his neighbor has fulfilled the law" (Rom. 13:8). After enumerating to the
Colossians the essential predicates of a good Christian—
mercy, kindness, humility, meekness, patience and forbear-
ance—he adds: "But above all these things have charity,
which is the bond of perfection" (Col. 3:14). "For the
whole law is fulfilled in one word: Thou shalt love thy
neighbor as thyself" (Gal. 5:14). Here he warns the Corinthians that marvels and prodigies will cease but that charity,

"the more excellent way" (13:1), will endure even throughout eternity when faith will flower into realization and hope flame up in fruition. Once again Paul's mind perfectly mirrors the mind of his Master, whose chief commandment was love of God and neighbor.

Read that "hymn to charity," as it has been called and see how genuinely Christian you are. Charity is patient, is kind; a divine concept surely in this day of snarling hatreds. Charity does not envy, is not pretentious or puffed up, is not ambitious or self-seeking; what a reversal of the values which so widely obtain in the world today, what an indictment of us who have fallen from these high principles. What is in your heart? Anger, cruelty, jealousy, pride, burning ambition, self-worship? That is the complete opposite of the Christian heart as Paul depicts it.

Take that passage on charity and for the word "charity" substitute the phrase "a Christian," and you will discover an accurate summary of what you should be. A *Christian* is kind, patient, not pretentious, and so for the rest. How do you measure up?

Put Away the Things of a Child

I Corinthians 13:11

Immaturity is that unbalanced state in which a man's attitude and actions have not yet overtaken his age. It would be humorous if it were not pitiable to see Edna Ferber's "gay old dog" trying to cheat the calendar and continue as a life-long collegian. Now, while a conventional latitude may be allowed a lady in the delicate matter of her age, it is always depressing to observe one with the physical appearance of grandmotherliness and the intellectual outlook of perennial girlishness. Moreover, the American colloquialism, "be your age!" is a curt rebuke to a man whose persistently youthful awkwardness belies his years. We have all met him—the man who is immature, socially, emotionally, intellectually or spiritually. The saddest sort of immaturity, however, is the last, as Saint Paul suggests by the comparison he uses in the epistle read on Quinquagesima Sunday.

"When I was a child," he writes to the Corinthians, "I spoke as a child, I felt as a child, I thought as a child. Now I have become a man, I have put away the things of a child." The first faltering steps of an infant, his initial attempts to speak, his utter dependence on others, his complete ignorance, are predicates which endear him to us. But in the nature of things they are temporary predicates, and if they perdure, if physical development hopelessly outstrips emotional and mental growth, if experience and educational opportunity accomplish little in the way of interior progress, then we recognize that the situation is, in greater or less degree, tragic. This holds in the spiritual life also: spiritual shallowness, lack of perception, infantile scales of value are to be expected in those who are beginners. But God and man alike have the right to expect growth, development, steady progress towards spiritual adulthood.

There is, of course, a spiritual childhood which Christ recommends to us: "Unless you . . . become like little children, you will not enter into the kingdom of heaven." But He immediately explains, pointing to the child before Him: "Whoever, therefore, humbles himself as this little child, he is the greatest in the kingdom of heaven" (Matt. 18:3). In other words, He places before us for our imitation the guilelessness, innocence, humility of the child. Paul endorses the sentiment when he exhorts the Corinthians: "Brethren, do not become children in mind, but in malice be children and in mind mature" (1 Cor. 14:20). Obviously, therefore, the admonition does not call for childishness, for religion in rompers, but for the innocence which results rather from conviction illumined by grace than from either inexperience or ignorance. Such was the "spiritual childhood" of the Little Flower, whose holiness was for a time so hideously sentimentalized by those who misunderstood it.

Talking to the Catholic Action youth of Rome, the Holy Father once pointed out the desperate need of such maturity. He inveighed against vague notions and mindless enthusiasm as modern substitutes for the clear principles they must have, called on them for great personal courage to face the bitter testing of their faith, demanded of them constant and consistent union between the faith they profess and the lives they live. In a letter to these United States, some nine years ago, he had insisted on the same need: "Our times require that the laity . . . procure for themselves a treasure of religious knowledge, not a poor and meager knowledge, but one that will have solidity and richness, through the medium of libraries, discussions and study clubs."

Yet many a man, determined to "get ahead," who studies to perfect himself in his profession, and practises for hours to improve even his putting, is content with the residual religious ideas, the half-forgotten truths of catechism classes attended long ago. He resents being called immature, even though in that most important realm of the spirit he has not yet "put away the things of a child."

Be Thou an Example to the Faithful

I Timothy 4:12

About this time every year a bell jangles somewhat rustily in the recesses of the Catholic conscience and the small reproachful voice whispers: "Lent is slipping away and you are scarcely noticing it. What have you given up? Nothing!" It is a nagging realization and, in a mild way which seldom induces action, it makes many a Catholic miserable.

Yet too many of us think of Lent only as a time when we should give something *up*; too few of us regard it as a season when we should *give* something. The self-denial which proceeds from love is not, after all, negative. Every time you give a present to a friend or loved one you deny yourself. You part with something. But the emphasis in such an action is scarcely negative.

Similarly, every time you make a decision; when you stand in a theatre of simultaneous possibilities, as William James grandly phrases it, and deliberately elect one over all others, you deny yourself to that degree. You cannot eat your cake and have it. Even the choice of a wife limits the man who, under God and in the light of Western civilization, has thrown over the harem theory. Nor does Bertrand Russell's sneer at monogamy as "intolerant, gross, cruel and hostile to all the best potentialities of human nature" make the ringing affirmation of the wedding morning a mere negation.

According to a pleasant anecdote, George M. Cohan once fell in with a crowd of Catholic gentlemen who had this self-torturing concept of Lent. One determined to give up his preprandial cocktail, another said he was giving up cigarettes, another chocolates, and so forth. Finally one of them turned to the Yankee-Doodle Dandy: "What are you giving up, George?" Mr. Cohan looked dourly around the heroic little circle and said sadly: "I'm just giving up." And many a Catholic, though he does not say so openly, does just that. Faced with the idea of mortification, he concentrates exclusively on the negative aspect of it, looks within himself and finds very little heroism; so he just gives up.

Yet everyone realizes at heart that some self-denial is necessary for sanity in the natural order as for salvation in the supernatural. Most thinking men would endorse this advice:

As a final practical maxim, relative to these habits of the will, we may, then, offer something like this: Keep the faculty of effort alive in you by a little gratuitous exercise every day. That is, be systematically ascetic or heroic in little, unnecessary points; do every day or two something for no other reason than that you would rather not do it . . . The man who has inured himself to habits of concentrated attention, energetic volition and self-denial in unnecessary things . . . will stand like a tower when everything rocks around him, and when his softer fellow-mortals are winnowed like chaff in the blast.

These words, which might be Saint Ignatius's gloss on his statement of the law of self-abnegation, are actually from William James's *Principles of Psychology*. Benjamin Franklin would agree with them no less than Epictetus; Leonidas would recognize their truth and Regulus and Chesterfield.

During the last war a short feature, with the then Captain Clark Gable as narrator, pictured the training of an Air Cadet. While the audience watched the officer candidates being put through a process of severest training in self-discipline and obedience, Captain Gable explained the reasons behind it. His explanation was a development of the text from Professor James. West Point and Annapolis are monuments to the same truth, that men and leaders cannot be made without a sculpturing of the soul that involves hammering, cutting, hard labor. And Lent, in the supernatural order, has the purpose of recalling to men, sharply and definitely, during a special season, that hard saying which it is easy and convenient to forget: ". . . unless you shall do penance, you shall all likewise perish." This is the testimony of logic as well as revelation.

When to the motivation of natural logic, however, one adds the stimulus of supernatural love, penance loses its negative connotations altogether. Blessed Henry Suso put his finger very near the heart of life when he observed that "love and suffering go together. There is no wooer but he is a sufferer; no lover but he is a martyr." It is necessary to discipline the lower nature that reason may not be unhorsed by unbridled animalism. But that is only part of the story. When one hears a Voice from beyond which calls: "If any man will be my disciple, let him take up his cross and come follow me," then, indeed, the "pawky maxims" of Poor Richard are swallowed in a challenge of love.

In his *Health and Holiness,* Francis Thompson waxed sarcastic about the softness of our modern generation. We are repelled at the idea of penance, he says, not because we are too self-indulgent but because we are too devitalized. Our pace of living is so hectic, our ganglia so constantly alerted by the alarms and excursions of modern life, that anything like heroic penance revolts us. Saint Teresa of Avila had made the same complaint in her *Life.*

But as a matter of fact, in our day one need not look far for the materials of penance and self-conquest. Millions of men who were in the service lived lives of daily self-contradiction, lives of Spartan mortification. Watching that Air Corps "short" which pictured the training of candidates, one could not help reflecting on that and hoping, moreover, that it was not mortification without motive and consequently, without merit. For the motive of the love of God can transmute any daily, grinding monotony into spiritual gold, just as the morning offering can sublimate all the actions of the day.

We who were wartime civilians felt the sting of privation, the itch of rationing, the burden of overwork, the ache of separation from loved ones; and many had heavier grief than this. Now as postwar civilians, we know the anxiety of uncertainty, the hardship of spiraling prices, shortages in basic necessities. "Great opportunities of serving God rarely offer themselves, but the little ones are always occurring," wrote Saint Francis de Sales, and he points out that little acts of love, a headache, a toothache and the like, "taken or accepted lovingly" can please God greatly. Calling "submission and obedience" the "penance of the reason," Saint John of the Cross affirms that such penance is more acceptable to God than acts of corporal penance. We can all offer that in greater or less degree.

Roehampton, the great Convent of the Sacred Heart in England, was, during the war, transformed into a hospital. One soldier-patient there read a lesson to his nurse in proper perspective and, incidentally, enunciated very strikingly the positive principle which should govern Lenten sacrifice. She was commiserating with him over the loss of his leg but he courteously and firmly rejected her sympathy. "I did not *lose* it," he insisted, "I *gave* it."

Behold, We Live, as Chastised

2 Corinthians 6:9

Between the burning Christianity of Saint Paul and the cold stoicism of his Roman contemporary, Seneca, there was literally a world of difference. But in one point of method, at least, they were agreed, as the epistle for the First Sunday of Lent indicates. Paul would have indorsed heartily Seneca's rule that teaching by theory is difficult and uncertain and that personal example is the brightest, most convincing advertisement of the truth.

His Divine Master had used the same approach to men's minds: "For I have given you an example, that as I have done to you, so you also should do" (John 13:15). It was fundamental in Paul's pedagogy: "that we might make ourselves an example for you to imitate us" (2 Thess. 3:10);

and he urged his apostolic associates to drive home their doctrines with their deeds: "be thou an example to the faithful" (1 Tim. 4:12) and, again, "show thyself in all things an example of good works" (Tit. 2:7). For the psychological fact is that men who can ignore a sublime precept find it hard to overlook a saint; they may condemn the mandate of God but any latent nobility is stirred and stimulated by a man of God.

Those early Christians were a light and a leaven in the world. "What force had the kingdom of souls at its disposal," asks Lacordaire, "against the empire armed with its legions?" Only the paradoxical weapons of their Divine Master, the scourge, contempt, crowning, crucifixion. "They had to conquer force, not by force, but by virtue." It was not for them merely to give abstract assent to the law of Christ but to reproduce, with the help of grace, the life of Christ in their own bodies.

In the original text, Paul simply declares "we conduct ourselves in all circumstances as God's ministers" but the present version changes the declarative to hortatory: *"Let us conduct* ourselves in all circumstances as God's ministers." The revision makes the text much more pointed on this first Sunday of Lent, for Paul is calling on you and me as well as the ancient Corinthians.

Our problem is much the same; we are still an embattled minority in a world of pagan carnival. The new paganism exalts the life of sense and sneers at the spirit; it makes self-repression synonymous with suffocation; it regards this earth as man's source and final destiny; it looks on a chaste heart as a rusty hearth choked with medieval ashes; it talks of love and means lust; its freedom is irresponsibility; it hails the literature of bathroom and bedroom, of prurience and even perversion as remarkably daring and advanced; vices are "values"; Christian reticence, retardation; modesty, mawkishness.

Against this mentality, the warning of Ash Wednesday, the challenge of Lent and Paul's desperate plea "not to receive the grace of God in vain" beat ineffectually. But it is our duty in a world of uplifted glass and unruly passion to walk as other Christs, to give the lie to the paganism around us by our lives, to let our light shine so that men may see our good works and at least think of our Father in Heaven. "Supposing that all who are Christians in name were Christians in fact," Clemenceau is reported to have said, "there would no longer be any social questions." If all were Christians in fact, many of our problems would be solved. "You who have the light, what are you doing with it?" asks Paul Claudel. Lent is a time for answering such questions, for self-examination, self-reformation.

In the Day of Salvation

2 Corinthians 6:2

A striking illustration of the power of grace is the story of the stormy, tenth-century John Gualbert, who dropped a murderer's dagger to become a monk and the founder of a famous monastery. John's brother Hugo had been killed and, in the vendetta code of those turbulent times in Florence, it devolved on John to vindicate Hugo's memory and avenge his death. Slowly he stalked his man, the nurtured hatred in his heart growing greater, until the day came when he finally overtook his quarry and squared off with him in a narrow lane.

According to one version of the story, it was Good Friday. Cold and merciless, he seized his brother's killer, threw him to the ground and dropped on him with the white dagger gleaming above the spread-eagled enemy. But, with his arms outflung, the sprawled man recalled to John the cross. One chronicler adds that as he momentarily faltered, he raised his eyes, and there, silhouetted against the sky, was the cross surmounting a church at the end of the lane. In any event, grace flooded and melted his heart, he dropped his knife and assisted his erstwhile foe to rise. On his way home, John paused for a visit in church, and his conversion was confirmed. He joined the Benedictines and went on to found the monastery and community of Vallombrosa.

The incident is compelling in itself and in its symbolism, as once again we stand on the threshold of Lent. For everything about this season should remind us of the cross; it leads to the cross, it is dominated by the cross. And that yearly revival of vision, that intensification of our spiritual lives which Lent calls for, should effect in us a definite change of heart, a minor conversion, a re-orienting of our lives, if perhaps they have detoured from the strait way that leads to salvation.

"The question 'how to live,'" wrote Matthew Arnold, "is the question which most interests every man, and with which, in some way or other, he is perpetually occupied." That question has been settled for us, in its broad outlines at least, by the life and death and resurrection of the historical Christ, by the deathless life of His infallible interpreter, the Mystical Christ, the Church. Our Lenten self-examination therefore is rather pointed at discovering how faithful we are to those divine directives.

We know them. We have chanted them glibly as children in catechism class. We have had them expounded, applied, particularized in the Catholic pulpit and press. We have renewed them in our reading. Our question is not so

much "how to live" but "how are we living?"—with what
fidelity to our faith, with what generosity towards God,
with what response to grace?

Lent is a time of special, spiritual opportunity. "He will
call upon me," says the Introit of the Mass for the first
Sunday of Lent; and then—to insist on the need of our
cooperative activity—it goes on, "and I will hear Him" (Ps.
90:15). The Collect drives home the equation between
divine generosity and human effort: "O God, who dost
purify thy Church by the yearly observance of Lent; grant
to thy household that what we strive to obtain from Thee
by abstinence we may secure by good works."

Saint Paul, in the epistle, lists some of his labors for
Christ, and points out that he carried himself blamelessly
"in tribulations, in hardships, in distresses; in stripes, in
imprisonments, in tumults; in labors, in sleepless nights;
. . . in kindness, in the Holy Spirit, in unaffected love."
Primary with him was his ministry, his love of Christ, compared to which his sufferings and labors were minor and
secondary indeed. So should it be with us, likewise.

We may not recognize ourselves in the tense figure of
John Gualbert, dagger in hand, advancing on his foe—
though, God knows, some of us harbor grudges and refuse
to forgive. But just as he was hagridden by a passion which
dominated his whole being, so we, too, have some pre-
dominant fault, sin or inclination which time after time
betrays us into infidelity. Lent, this very Lent, is a season
of grace and salvation. John Gualbert had his day of salvation. He accepted the grace of God. This season is given
to us, and because of our gift of liberty, at once divine and
dangerous, we can make the triumphant choice of John

Gualbert or the tragic mistake of Judas Iscariot. That decision faces man day after day; he is helped by reason and revelation, by grace habitual and actual, but he is not coerced into beatitude.

The Will of God, Your Sanctification

I Thessalonians 4:3

To one who, like Henry James, delights "in a palpable, imaginable, visitable past," the name Thessalonica rings like a hammer on an anvil. For centuries that city, now called Salonika, has been a teeming port, host or target for navies, focus of sieges, a strategic prize. Vital roads fanned out from it, an enclosed harbor lay before it; it dominated the imperial life-line between Rome and her Eastern possessions in such wise that Cicero, who spent part of his exile there, spoke of the Thessalonians as "placed in the lap of the Empire." Not the least of its titles to respect is that to the early Christians there Saint Paul wrote two of his epistles. A fragment of the first is read in the Mass for the second Sunday of Lent.

When he arrived at Thessalonica, Paul found many Jews working in the busy weaving marts, and for three successive Sabbaths he vainly addressed himself to them. Finding them obdurate in their refusal of Christ, he turned to the pagans, who were surprisingly receptive, and it was these converts whom he sustained and strengthened by his two letters. They were taking their first faltering steps in the faith, they were living in a city of sin, temptation was strong and none knew better than Paul that man is weak. The letters remind them of his doctrine and implore them to embrace the moral obligations deriving from those truths.

There is an attitude abroad today, a comfortable conviction which small souls cherish, that restricted service, half-hearted love are sufficient return to Christ for all that He did for us. The part-time Catholic keeps his religion strictly departmentalized within the half-hour he allots to it on Sunday morning; he makes his Easter duty but is generally too busy to confess and receive frequently; he has no time in the morning to dedicate the day to God; he is too weary in the evening to say his night prayers; he is not above sharp practice in business; he habitually commits deliberate venial sins and occasionally falls into mortal faults; but, withal, he feels he is doing enough. He is "not a monk (or a nun)," he tells you, but "a man of the world, a practical man."

Paul had no intention of letting his converts lapse into this rationalized mediocrity. You have done well, he assures them encouragingly, but you must keep on. "We beseech and exhort you in the Lord Jesus to make even greater progress." In the life of the spirit it is axiomatic that not to advance is to go back. "A man," says Pope Gregory the Great, "falls to the bottom unless he strives to reach the top." So Paul bluntly tells them and us that God is not satisfied with a small return on His great investment of love: "This is the will of God, your sanctification."

All around his converts was temptation; animalism and loose morality threatened the new ideal of Christian chastity within marriage and outside of it. Lust, Paul warns them, must not be permitted to ravage the body and regulate one's life; the battle against passion has no armistice, admits of no quarter; we must continually fight and so "please God."

The breakdown of our public morality reflected in the lurid headlines of the public press; in the decadent taste, creative and critical, in literature, points out to us how timeless and therefore timely are the Pauline admonitions.

Yet parents permit children to stock immature imaginations with foul pictures from movie, magazine or "comic books"; mothers elevate vogue above virtue and allow daughters to dress immodestly at the dictate of inexorable fashion. Many parents are more casual about chastity than the saints dared to be. "No chastity," says the *Imitation*, "is secure if you do not protect it."

There are heedless parents who see no harm in the game of chance that their children play with loose, careless spirituality. A child falls into sinful habits not because of any need of nature but because of morbid thinking, and by reading books, seeing movies of carnal allure, by seeking evil environment. Timeless and timely is the voice of Saint Paul, vibrant with the wisdom of Christ: "You know what precepts I have given to you by the Lord Jesus. For this is the will of God, your chastity, your holiness, your honor, your sanctification." Saint Paul is not satisfied with mediocre spirituality. That kind of spirituality is half-hearted. Neither should parents be satisfied. With fullness of heart they must seek God—go forward, make greater progress as militant Catholics in the battle against sin.

Immorality Not Even Named among You

Ephesians 5:3

The epistles of the Second and Third Sundays of Lent are loud with Saint Paul's denunciations of impurity, and one might wonder at the Church's strong, successive insistence on the point. An obvious explanation is that the holy season of Lent requires the repressing of the flesh and the exaltation of the spirit, the chastisement of the body to "bring it into subjection" (1 Cor. 9:27) under threat of eternal rejection.

Certainly no one can deny now the appropriateness of today's quotation from the Epistle to the Ephesians. One need only think of the radio comedian with his double-barreled suggestiveness, the bawdier type of picture magazine which has relieved its patrons even of the burden of reading captions, the advertisements which make paging through a newspaper an adventure perilous for the pure soul, the commercial blurbs depicting the body beautiful and, by implication, the soul benighted. Just the opposite is the spirit of Lent, which calls for the soul beautiful and the body de-emphasized, disciplined, reminded of its origins by the ashes on its brow, reduced to docility by penance.

Concupiscence (scientifically renamed to be sure) smolders in our souls, continually fanned by the false ideas breathing through modern society. Our whole education, says C. S. Lewis, "tends to fix our minds on this world"; but Lent reminds us that we walk here as aliens, exiles, pilgrims who must not become entranced with the road but press on eagerly to the glowing goal.

Ephesus, when Paul wrote his letter, was the great commercial center of Asia Minor, renowned for its Temple of Diana, one of the marvels of the antique world. Before the Ephesians, living in this tainted atmosphere, Paul places Jesus Christ through whom the Father's eternal plan was actualized, by whom they were raised to spiritual life, to whom they were united in unimaginable intimacy. That being so, they had to divest themselves of those vices which could frustrate the divine plan for them, quench the divine life in them; and Paul enumerates some of those sins.

They must flee immorality of whatever kind, chain the beast within them. Obscenity in deed or word will destroy them spiritually. The "foolish talking" which Paul mentions means not merely babbling gossip but the external expression of an unchaste mind. For the worship of the flesh, which he calls "idolatry," brings down the "wrath of God."

We of the modern world might well make an examination of conscience along the lines here suggested. Our morality is under constant pressure; we have seen marriage degraded to the status of a temporary legalized liaison lightly to be dissolved; cartoonists and "gag men" have explored and exploited its humorous possibilities. We have seen it become almost accepted custom to tell stories which are suggestive if not actually rancid. The learned have supplied sonorous synonyms for lust and have assured man of his right to shape his life according to his lower instincts.

It is heartening to note that many Catholics all over the land often renew their marriage vows as a concrete protest against the burlesque of matrimony. Originally planned as a local observance of the Family Life Conference in Chicago, the idea has won nationwide enthusiasm. But that is not enough. One boulder will not halt a flood; we need a high, deep, strong dam of decency against the torrent of rottenness which hell has loosed upon the world. It needs many hands, many hearts to build such a barrier; and such hearts must be pure, such hands white, with the light of holiness which makes us "children of light." "For you were once darkness," Paul tells us, "but now you are light in the Lord."

Rejoice with Joy

The Introit

Laetare Sunday is another instance of the essential, irrepressible joy bubbling up from the heart of our holy faith and overflowing even in a season of penitence. Father Martindale, writing on the liturgy, declares: "The Catholic religion is meant to be a happy one," and again "the liturgy of the Church is full of the notion of joy." In the epistle for today's Mass, Saint Paul gives what is perhaps the basic reason for inextinguishable Christian happiness, and that is the great liberty which the faith gives us. Free men are happy men; and the faith of Christ is the faith of freedom.

That remark will shock or amuse those enemies of the Church who are forever portraying her as a hopeless reactionary, shackling the souls of her children with prohibitions, opposing progress, stuck fast in the medieval mud. But it will strike a responsive chord in the hearts of converts who, often contrary to their own expectation, have found freedom in the Church and have recorded their discovery.

Speaking of his conversion, Albert Von Ruville summed it all up in the relieved sigh: "Now at last I am free." Robert Hugh Benson, Gilbert K. Chesterton and Ronald Knox are only a few who have similarly reacted. "I have been overwhelmed with the feeling of liberty," wrote Monsignor Knox, "the glorious liberty of the sons of God." They and thousands of others have come to appreciate what Saint Jerome meant, in his commentary on Isaias: "For the Lord is a Spirit; and where the Spirit of the Lord is, there is liberty"—words taken from Saint Paul (2 Cor. 3:17). That same sense of liberation illuminates Clare Booth Luce's account of her conversion: it is the deep foundation of Christian joy.

Paul's somewhat involved passage is directed at the Judaizers, a vexatious group in the early Church who contended that the Jewish Christians were still bound by the Mosaic Law, that all the legal apparatus of the Old Dispensation should be engrafted on the New. Such were the Pharisees described by Saint Luke, who, though they had accepted the faith, still said of other converts: "They must be circumcised and also told to observe the Law of Moses" (Acts 15:5). Against them Paul vindicated the liberty of the New Law.

He contrasts the Old Law and the New, typifying them by persons of the Old Testament, Agar, the slave, mother of Ismael (Gen. 16), and Sara, the free woman, mother of Isaac (Gen. 21). He compares the local, earthly Jerusalem, capital of the Jewish race, with the all-embracing heavenly Jerusalem, the Church. Against the Jews, bondsmen to the Law of Moses, he sets the Christians, free under the gospel and faith of Christ.

Centuries before, Isaias (61:1) foretold that the Messiah would come "to set at liberty the oppressed" (Luke 4:19). Saint James refers to Christ's law simply as "the perfect law of liberty" (James 1:25); it was a constant theme with Paul: "For you have been called to liberty, brethren" (Gal. 5:13). Christ freed us from sin (Rom. 6:18) and so from the deep-rooted fear of damnation; He freed us from want, by pouring out upon us His Blood and the "abundant riches of His grace" (Eph. 2:7). He gave us Heaven, hope, love, confident assurance.

The sound political principle which makes eternal vigilance the price and condition of liberty obtains in the spiritual order too. There is the slavery of sin whereby a man delivers himself, bound hand and foot, to passion and evil habits. He may try to find happiness in a bottle, in money, in the wrong kind of friendships, in dishonesty. But only in the Lord will he discover real joy, boundless liberty; only in the Lord can he really accept the invitation of the Introit of Laetare Sunday: "Rejoice with joy, you that have been in sorrow."

The Ransom He Has Won Lasts Forever

Hebrews 9:12

Montalembert once made a meditation and drew a conclusion most appropriate for Passion Sunday. "If it could be granted to us," he wrote, "to have lived at the time when Jesus lived in this world and to see Him for only one moment, we should have chosen that moment when He was on His way, crowned with thorns and bent with weariness, to Calvary." That is the vision of Christ which should possess our hearts and minds on Passion Sunday and during the declining days of Lent. The liturgy dramatically intensifies the spirit of mourning; purple drapes hide all statuary; certain prayers are suppressed in the Holy Sacrifice; a deep sadness pervades the day.

Representations of the suffering Christ which portray

Him as immaculately immune from blood, sweat and tears, serve neither art nor accuracy. The Passion was an ugly, brutal business and we can get no adequate idea of it if we insist on imagining only an ivory Christ on a mahogany cross. The Man who stumbled wearily along the first Way of the Cross was a pitiable sight. His back was flayed from the scourging, the thorns dug deep into His head, the roughhewn beams of the cross lacerated His shoulder and hacked His heels, thrice tripping Him and throwing Him heavily. Each breath was a battle and an agony; thirst consumed Him, fever burned in His veins.

At Bethlehem He had "emptied Himself, taking the nature of a slave and being made like unto men" (Phil. 2:7). But at Bethlehem and during His life previous to the Passion, He was the most beautiful of the sons of men. Now love drives Him to the ultimate sacrifice which makes of Him "a worm and no man" (Ps. 21:7) "despised, and the most abject of men, a man of sorrows" (Isaias 53:3).

It is this Victim and High Priest, Christ the Redeemer, whom Paul presents to us in the section from Hebrews which is read as the epistle of the Passion Sunday Mass. Writing to the converts from the Old Law, Paul points out to them the immeasurable superiority of the New. We are sanctified and redeemed, he assures them, not by the blood of goats or oxen but by the blood of Christ.

That picture of Christ dying on the cross, silhouetted against a black sky, crying "I thirst" through parched and twisted lips, was always before Paul. He knew that worldly sophistication laughed the cross to scorn, that human weakness quailed before its implications. "For the doctrine of the cross is foolishness to those who perish, but to those who are saved, that is, to us, it is the power of God." (I

Cor. 1:18). It was always "a crucified Christ" whom Paul preached and, despite all his learning, his great gifts of mind and power of expression, he assured the Corinthians: "For I determined not to know anything among you, except Jesus Christ and Him crucified" (I Cor. 2:2).

With uncomfortable directness, therefore, Passion Sunday places before us the cross, a stark reminder that Jesus who loved us so much expects a return of that love. How little of the heroic there is in most of us. Yet Christ is most explicit; "he who does not carry his cross and follow me, cannot be my disciple" (Luke 14:27). Make the Stations of the Cross one of these days, pause long and lovingly at each stage on Christ's last mile and ask yourself: Where am I in all this? Following afar off, like Peter? Hidden in the safe anonymity of the mob or courageous with Veronica? Far from the cross or sharing it intimately as Simon did?

God Also Has Exalted Him

Philippians 2:9

Palm Sunday is the feast-day of the superficial and the vociferous, those whose lives do not square with their protestations, who are enthusiastic about appearances but unable logically to think through to the realities and significances which underlie surfaces. So it was with the travelers from every section of the Roman Empire who were jammed into Jerusalem for the coming festival of the Pasch, the very morning when the news spread from lip to lip, "Jesus of Nazareth is approaching the city with His disciples. He is the great teacher, the wonder-worker."

Most of the Jews knew Him, even those who had come from afar and, carried off their feet by unthinking fervor, they rushed out to meet Him. The crowds who had listened

to His sermons and the clear development of His doctrine
were attentive multitudes. But the screaming throng of
Palm Sunday was a mindless mob, swept along by slogans.

This, to a casual observer, was the greatest triumph of
Christ's life. Though the thousands had been in admiration
of His teaching (Mark 6:2), though once they had come
to take Him by force and make Him their king (John
6:15), the acclamation of Palm Sunday was far greater
than any previous public demonstration. Yet it was utterly
meaningless and served only to highlight in greater irony
the strident verdict which these same throats would shriek
in five short days: "Crucify Him."

His miracles and His fearless opposition to the entrenched
and hypocritical leaders of the people had endeared Him
to the crowds. They looked on Him as the mighty Messiah
who would drive out the hated Roman and restore Israel
to a prominent place in the sun, re-establishing them not
in the spiritual but material position of honor. On this first
Palm Sunday, their hopes seemed ready for fulfillment.

Saint Paul, in the epistle of the Mass, indicates the real
glory of Palm Sunday. This Man around whom the shout-
ing populace swayed and surged was on His way not to
a crown or a throne but to "death, even to death on a
cross." As He entered the city on a donkey, the Jews should
have recognized Him, because Isaias and Zachary had foretold that their King would be "meek" and seated on "a
colt, the foal of a beast of burden." But they did not want
a mild Messiah; their hearts were set on a militant, flashing
leader who would found an earthly kingdom. And so on
Friday, when they saw Him bound, beaten, derided, wordless and will-less before His tormentors, they turned on
Him. When He had prestige and power they exalted Him;

but when He was a voluntary Victim, obedient unto death, "God . . . exalted him and bestowed upon him the name that is above every name."

We, too, like the variable crowds in the first Holy Week, can become confused in our scale of values. We hear Christ say "Learn of me because I am meek and humble of heart" (Matt. 24:32) but, like the ancient Jews, we can condemn meekness in our own hearts and perform constantly actions which are the overflow of arrogance. "Unless you do penance you shall all likewise perish" (Luke 13:3), He admonishes us; but our lives are monumentally self-indulgent. We are happy to follow Him on Palm Sunday, as the apostles did, glorying in His triumph; but in Gethsemane our hearts and eyelids are alike heavy; Calvary is too high to climb, the cross too rough to embrace. By Good Friday the bright, green palms of Sunday's reception were withered and brittle; they might well symbolize our spiritual resolutions.

Read the Passion again, lovingly and penetratingly. Through His sufferings Jesus redeemed us; in His sufferings He gave us an example. Our spirit is willing but our flesh, like that of Peter, James and John, is weak. We must watch and pray and make our own the muscular prayer of Saint Ignatius: "Passion of Christ, strengthen me."

Let Us Keep Festival

I Corinthians 5:8

One hears a great deal these days about the beginning of a new era, an atomic age, born of the blasts over Hiroshima and Nagasaki. It was, we are told, the most impressive release of power in man's history. In the fearsome presence of the genie of smoke standing over Bikini, man must search his heart, readjust his thinking, re-examine his cherished convictions.

This is all very true; but, centuries ago there was darkness over the earth one afternoon and an earthquake shook the world to its roots, riving the hill called Golgotha. Centuries ago, one Sunday morning, a second earthquake rolled the stone from a tomb, out of which Jesus Christ,

judicially murdered on Friday, walked in triumph. These
world-shaking convulsions were infinitely more powerful
than anything at Hiroshima, Nagasaki or Bikini. From that
empty sepulchre there came the force which would revo-
lutionize the world, conquer the invincible Roman Empire
through the quiet campaigns of conversion and energize
the hearts and souls of men until the end of time.

A new era was inaugurated, the Christian epoch, self-
renewing, self-perpetuating. "The earth trembled and was
still," says the Offertory of the Easter Mass, "when God
arose in judgment." In these days of atomic horror which
remind man so frequently of his death, it is comforting to
meditate for a moment on his deathlessness, too. For Easter
gave life a new meaning.

It is, in its very concept, a feast of renewal, or revival,
a reminder and a guarantee of our own immortality. The
resplendent Christ, victorious over disgrace and death, is
an assurance to us that we are "sons of God . . . and heirs
also: heirs indeed of God and joint heirs with Christ, provided, however, we suffer with him that we may also be
glorified with him" (Rom. 8:17). In that final proviso,
Paul insists again on the causal connection between the
cross and the crown, between a share in Christ's anguish
and a part in His glory.

We must be one with Him in "the fellowship of his
sufferings" and so, as the saint says, "become like to him
in death, in the hope that somehow I may attain to the
resurrection from the dead" (Phil. 3:10, 11) "For if we
believe that Jesus died and rose again, so with him God
will bring those also who have fallen asleep through Jesus"
(1 Thess. 4:14). The real Catholic therefore has no morbid
fear of death nor does he grieve inconsolably over his dear

ones who have passed from his arms through the gate of the grave into the arms of Our Lord.

In the spirit of Paschal renewal and revival, Paul, in the epistle of the Mass, calls for a renovation within our own individual souls. Writing his first letter to the Corinthians, he chides them because there was a man living among them guilty of unnatural immorality. The presence of such, he says, is a diabolic leaven or yeast which could corrupt the whole mass, and he subjoins the command which is the opening line of the Easter epistle: "Purge out the old leaven, that you may be a new dough."

As we look into our own souls, that ancient exhortation still has point. We find there vicious inclinations, unconquered habits of sin, old hatreds and resentments, dishonesty, hypocrisy. They are the old leaven which we must purge out lest their fermentation, their pervading decay should disease the whole soul. Against the soul internally agitated by the fermentation of sin, Paul contrasts "the unleavened bread of sincerity and truth." He means a spirit which despises interior immorality of whatever kind, no less than that superficial, external respectability which is a cloak for internal insincerity.

So on Easter morning, consider your faith as well as your fashion. Do not let all your concern be for those who will look at your hat so that you forget Him who looks at your heart. He is "our Passover," the Paschal Lamb of God who took away the sins of the world. Do your actions sneer at His sacrifice? Does your life give Him the lie?

The Victory That Overcomes the World, Our Faith

I John 5:4

If anything is evident from Saint John's Gospel and Epistles, it is the irreconcilable hostility between Christ and the world, an opposition apparent in the epistle for Low Sunday, most frighteningly clear in Christ's own blunt words: "not for the world do I pray" (John 17:9). Dreadful indeed must be that evil which lies in the lightless, loveless desert outside of Christ's prayer. We should know definitely what the "world" and "worldliness" really mean, lest we subscribe to them and so place our souls in the exterior darkness of exile.

A man may be in the world, Saint Thomas Aquinas teaches, in two senses: by his mere bodily presence or, in addition, by the gravitation and inclination of his heart and mind. In that first meaning we are all obviously in the world. The spiritual danger is that we should be in it in the second sense, that our hearts, minds, hopes and loves should be bounded by the horizons of time and the transient. The apostles were in the world in the physical sense: "These are in the world, and I am coming to Thee" (John 17:11). But previously in the same discourse Christ had made it clear that though they were *in* the world, they were by no means to be *of* the world: "I have chosen you out of the world" (John 15:19).

Similarly we must constantly recall that we are "pilgrims and strangers on earth . . . that we seek after a better, that is, a heavenly country" (Heb. 11:13, 16). We must "mind the things that are above, not the things that are on earth" (Col. 3:2), and "use this world as though not using it" (1 Cor. 7:31). As we walk the way of pilgrimage through this alien land to our true homeland, heaven, we are guided and strengthened by grace, but our free wills are wobbly and variable, easily seduced and allured by the creatures we encounter. "The soul cannot live without loving," Catherine of Siena wrote, "and it all depends on what we love."

Unfortunately, the human heart can anchor itself so completely in and to the world as to be unable to rise to the Author of the world. The creatures we encounter were designed by God to help us back to Him. Nevertheless we can abuse them, misuse them, turn them to purposes other than those God intended. In the divine plan they are stepping-stones to Him, but our obscured minds and vicious wills can make of them stumbling-blocks. They are bridges to carry us to God, but the treacherous heart can readily change them into barriers.

The danger is very real. Cardinal Newman states it well: "Look not about for the world as some vast and gigantic evil far off—its temptations are close to you, apt and ready, suddenly offered and subtle in their address. Try to bring down the words of Scripture to common life, and to recognize the evil in which this world lies, in your own hearts." The human heart has a short-sighted tendency to fasten on the here, the now, the tangible. This urge must be regulated by reason and revelation, as Saint John says: "This is the victory that overcomes the world, our faith" (I John 5:4).

"Do not love the world," he elsewhere insists, "or the things that are in the world. If anyone loves the world, the love of the Father is not in him; because all that is in the world is the lust of the flesh, and the lust of the eyes, and the pride of life" (1 John 2:16).

Here is the genesis of all sin, Aquinas says. The lust of the flesh urges man to carnal satisfaction. The lust of the eyes is aroused by the glitter of possessions. The pride of life drives man to desire the estimation and applause of men, to seek position and to gain prestige. That is the spirit of the world, which should be as loathsome to us as it was to Christ.

An Example That You May Follow

I Peter 2:21

Pain, moral, physical or mental, is the marplot in all utopias: the mystery of human misery is the specter haunting those philosophies which hold that man, through endless evolutionary improvements, can emerge as superman. Yet, even as the thinker spins his theories of our competence to slough infirmity and rise robust, he, himself, wan and worn at his task, may well be forced to lay aside his pen and his purpose. It is with adhesive reluctance that we turn from the possibility of excising pain to the necessity of enduring it. Unless we have a strong motive to insulate us against discouragement and despair, we can readily rebel. Such a motive must be supernatural. Its cause and nature are indicated often in the Scriptures, and one an-

nouncement of it occurs in the section of Saint Peter's first
epistle, read in the Mass for the second Sunday after Easter.

Peter's apostolate had carried him through Pontus, Ga-
latia, Cappadocia, Asia and Bithynia. In those provinces
he had converted many of the scattered Jews. Surrounded
by hostility and all kinds of spiritual and physical hardship, the neophytes made their first steps along a high,
hard road.

Writing from Rome, which he metaphorically terms
"Babylon," the first Pope encourages his charges and calls
them to heroic fidelity. His letter, loud with echoes from
the prophet of the Passion, Isaias, reminds them and us to
look back on Calvary, to remember that we "have been
bought at a great price" (I Cor. 6:20), "that through many
tribulations we must enter the kingdom of God" (Acts
14:21). He addresses himself to the different classes of
society in Asia Minor, and the passage read in this morning's
Mass is intended for the slaves whose cruel lot was all too
likely to make them heirs of hopelessness: "Christ has
suffered for us, leaving you an example," Peter writes, "that
you may follow in His steps."

The reasoning is simple: Several times had Peter heard
his Divine Master enunciate the principle: "No disciple
is above his teacher, nor is the servant above his master. It
is enough for the disciple to be like his teacher and for the
servant to be like his master" (Matt. 10:24, 25), a norm
which Our Lord twice repeated at the Last Supper. Christ
had never given the impression that it was easy to follow
Him.

In the first full statement of His teaching He had declared that suffering persecution for "justice sake" was a
title to blessedness; and to the traditional eight, there is

subjoined what might be called a ninth Beatitude: "Blessed are you when men reproach you, and persecute you and, speaking falsely, say all manner of evil against you, for my sake. Rejoice and exult, because your reward is great in heaven" (Matt. 5:11). Peter had learned well: he it was who led the Apostles in their rejoicing "that they had been counted worthy to suffer disgrace for the name of Jesus" (Acts 5:41).

So now he writes to these slaves: surely you have suffered, but not nearly as scaldingly as the sinless Lord. You are reviled, but He was engulfed in a cascade of opprobrium and contempt. You are treated unjustly, but He was murdered in a judicial farce. He has given you so much that all you can offer will be small return indeed. That is the mentality which, under grace, makes saints. Saints are men who sublimated and canonized their pains, anxieties, worries; who saw in these grim visitations the opportunity to be more like Christ, a motive which makes life not only bearable but joyous. They faced difficulty not with the stolid endurance of fatalism but the happy acceptance of faith. And we, who in our mediocrity are forever murmuring, must learn the same lesson and drive bitterness from our hearts, rebelliousness from our wills by imitating the example of the Master.

Honor All Men

I Peter 2:17

Fortitude is a fine, muscular word with the hard outline and impact of a fist. It jolts the memory to recall Perpetua and Felicitas, patrician and peasant, united as sisters in the democracy of faith and death; Ambrose, Augustine and Chrysostom defending the truth despite hostile troops, threats and exile; Miguel Pro smiling at the rifle barrels and crumpling in death with a chivalrous salute to Christ the King.

Fortitude is necessary in the natural order, as moral philosophers from Aristole to William James have insisted. Moreover, in its fullness, fortitude signifies not only a cardinal virtue but a gift of the Holy Spirit: the inflexible and courageous adherence to the truth which resides in a soul suffused and stiffened by grace. As such it is extremely important in our supernatural armament, and Popes from Peter to Pius have pointed that out. The first epistle of the first Pope, a part of which is read in the Mass for the Third Sunday after Easter, is a thrilling call to fortitude in his converts in Asia Minor.

It was no easy program that Peter outlined for these ancient spiritual ancestors of ours. Hostile eyes bored into them, misconstruing their motives, misinterpreting their mode of life. Calumny, oppression, physical violence were their daily experiences.

Yet he exhorts them to walk untainted by the foulness which washed around them, to give that example which would be the best advertisement of their faith and would induce in their pagan confreres something of a predisposition for the coming of grace. As citizens they are to be models in their fulfillment of civic obligation, looking through the person in authority to see behind him the God from whom legitimate authority flows. Towards their fellows, pagan or Christian, they are to conduct themselves humbly and deferentially. But for their Christian brothers, as members of the same Mystical Christ, they are to have special devotion and affection. Before God they must have that filial reverence and awe which His transcendent holiness demands.

In four brief admonitions, therefore, Peter spans all the obligations of a Christian: "Honor all men; love the brotherhood; fear God; honor the king." And in the same vein of humility and obedience he commands servants to submission even though their masters be severe.

It is a picture of high holiness and heroic fortitude which Saint Peter places before his flock and it well might give us pause. We insist on having our religion softened and made more palatable for us; we recoil automatically from the heroic. Even the ordinary inescapable slings and arrows of living annoy us beyond the enduring, as Saint Teresa of Avila said about her contemporaries and Francis Thompson about his.

It is largely the virtue and gift of fortitude which can change us. There was no one in the history of souls who realized that better than Peter himself. In Gethsemane, in the courtyard of the High Priest, on the outer fringes of the crowd at Calvary, he had learned in the bitter school of sin and tears his own weakness. But on Pentecost he had been strengthened "with power from on high" (John 24:49), he had been "strengthened with power through his Spirit unto the progress of the inner man" (Eph. 3:16).

The Paschal season is alive with Pentecostal rustlings as we recall the vigil of the apostles awaiting the visitation of the Paraclete. The same Holy Spirit broods over us willing and able to give us the fortitude to walk untouched by the paganism of our day: good Catholics, good citizens, lovers of Christ, unshaken by trial or temptation, upright, honest, sincere.

Every Good Gift from Above

James 1:17

Changeless permanence is a notion which has always fascinated man at the same time that it has defied him. Build as he will, deep foundation and mighty pillar, he knows that the seeping trickle will melt his mortar; that the small, insistent grass will at last conquer his piled granite; that the slumbering ground will arch its back in earthquake and topple his marble immortalities. He knows that all his works, sooner or later, will join Shelley's statue of Ozymandias beneath the drifting sands. Too seldom does man look for immutability in that One Being in whom, as Saint James reminds us in the epistle for the fourth Sunday after Easter, "there is no change, nor shadow of alteration."

But as the saint assures us, God is not just an aloof and

inaccessible Being—Herbert Spencer's "Supreme Energy" or Shailer Matthews' "personality-producing force"—but a loving parent, "the Father of Lights." He is the fountainhead of those supernatural gifts, those graces which elevate us to the breathless dignity of a real though limited participation in the Divine Nature and to divine sonship, with all that implies. This all-loving Father has "begotten us by the word of truth," and the idea of paternity is here no mere figure of speech but an accurate description of wondrous fact. There was no merit, however slight, in us which brought us this marvelous endowment of divine sonship. It was utterly and completely God's gratuitous mercy, as Saint Peter, employing the same idea of rebirth, is careful to point out: "Blessed be the God and Father of our Lord Jesus Christ, who according to his great mercy has begotten us through the resurrection of Jesus Christ from the dead." Then, to show us that the reward awaiting us will share in the unchanging loveliness of God, he adds: "unto an incorruptible inheritance—undefiled and unfading, reserved for you in heaven" (1 Peter 1:3, 4).

Truly, in a world of shifting certitudes and transient loyalties, God alone is "the changeless Friend," who not only wishes us well but has the omnipotence to bring His wishes to glorious fulfillment, if only we will not thwart them by our perversity. Yet we who talk so much about "rainy days" in the future, so often forget that only in Him, through Him and by Him can we attain the unalterable happiness which is the deepest dream of the restless human heart.

That Saint James was fully aware of our fickleness and faint-heartedness is clear from the trenchant contrast which his letter presents. In a few swift phrases he characterizes

God, the infinitely bountiful giver, benevolent, paternally loving. Against His ineffable majesty he places man, moody, undependable, reluctant to listen, eager to speak, quick to quarrel, inclined to wrath, with "uncleanness and abundance of malice." The soul shaken by the constant tumult of the senses, soured by resentments or slimed with sensuality and uncharitableness is not a proper subject for God's saving action. Saint James therefore calls on us to remove these obstacles and to cultivate the climate of meekness which alone is the right atmosphere for "the engrafted word, which is able to save your souls."

The "word," of course, is redemptive truth and grace and, by calling it engrafted (or implanted, another possible translation), Saint James insists again that it is not a natural outgrowth, that it is not something due us but that it is superadded through God's munificence.

The picture of man in this epistle is an embarrassingly accurate likeness for each of us to contemplate. Saint James has adroitly drawn an image of the soul of the sinful man who was once made to the image and likeness of God, the "Father of Lights." Every true son bears a likeness to his father. And it is to a restoration of divine likeness that Saint James urges us. Man is the noblest of all the creatures of God and the only man without nobility is the man who has destroyed in his own soul the image of God, the Father, engrafted by the Word of God to the soul of man on the Tree of Calvary.

Be Doers of the Word

James 1:22

Characteristic of our tendency to solemnize the trivial and snub the significant is the fact that we who so roundly disdain lukewarmness in our soups so readily condone it in our souls. As a spiritual predicate, lukewarmness means an anesthesia of spirit, a torpor of soul and slumbering neutrality which cannot be awakened to any active allegiances, is allergic to any motivation however sublime, and is loyal only to the negative gods of lethargy.

As Dante and Virgil entered the Inferno they discovered, close inside the grim gates, a whole host of spirits who during their lives, had "lived without blame and without praise." The poet of ancient Rome told the poet of dogmatic Rome that these people were forever allied with the angels who, when Lucifer raised revolt in heaven, "were not rebellious, nor were faithful to God; but were for themselves." Living neither in heaven nor in hell, these spirits, fiercely goaded by hornets and wasps, were forever condemned to pursue a banner because in their somnolent lives they had never embraced a cause. It is a poetical description of the lukewarm, the spiritually inert, whose only motion is drifting, whose only ambition is disengagement.

Extreme as that may seem, there are still many Catholics whom the description fits, as Saint James intimates in the epistle for the Fifth Sunday after Easter. They hear the word of God. They are vaguely attracted by its beauty, but they refuse to reduce it to action. In the gospel, as in a mirror, they see the reflection of the ideal Christian, but they go away and forget that challenging image. Almost every Sunday such people attend the Holy Sacrifice. They come late and leave early. Almost every year they perform their Easter duty at the last hour. For the rest of the year, they keep religion severely one of life's minor concerns.

Content with themselves, they regard habitual venial sin without alarm and even shrug off with great tolerance occasional mortal sin. If it serves their purpose they tell lies, while reserving the right to resent being called liars. The principles and truths of religion to which they pay lip service on Sunday are left carefully in church, because these hinder their unscrupulous practices in business on Monday.

Many of them are genteel anticlericals. On occasion they are fiercely and unintelligently critical of priests who are engaged in activities that offend their complacency. Totally unaware of the Church's carefully propounded position on labor problems, education, marriage and even such matters as planned parenthood, they have the sometimes articulate suspicion that the Church would do well to stay behind her altar-rail.

Now religion is not merely the embracing of a set of bloodless principles. It is an operative love for a person—the Divine Person of the Eternal Word, Our Lord Jesus Christ. If ever there was a life marked by a singleness of purpose and an inextinguishable ardor which is an immortal reproach to lukewarmness, that life was His. From His first recorded utterance, which dedicated His life to the Father's business (Luke 2:49), down to the declining moments of His final agony, when He announced the completion of His mission (John 19:30), His days were consumed by a tireless love. The cry which has twisted the hearts of saints for centuries was the tortured "I thirst" (John 19:28). While we know that He burned with bodily thirst, we realize that His real fever was His mystical desire for our love. Lukewarmness, the tepid return of a spiritually arid life to Him who did so much for us and died for us, is an insult.

Saint James holds the mirror up to us this morning. Look into it frankly—without delusion or self-deception—and see your heart as God sees it. Do you see mirrored there God's workman, the doer of His word or do you see God's weakling, the listless hearer of His law? Indeed, we can with great profit look into our hearts as Saint James suggests in this morning's epistle—"For if anyone is a hearer of the word and not a doer, he is like a man looking at his natural face in a mirror: for he looks at himself and goes away and presently forgets what kind of man he is. But he who has looked carefully,—he shall be blessed" and his heart shall be pure and undefiled and unspotted.

Above All Things Have Mutual Charity

I Peter 4:8

Humanitarianism is one of those ritualistic words which, in our day, have reduced the burden of thought by substituting vague phrases with indefinable connotations and elusive overtones for clean, hard concepts. As an historical movement, humanitarianism, or positivism, is subject to definition; but in its popular usage in press and forum, it covers a multitude of meanings. The least its exponents would claim for it is that humanitarianism is a system which features man by emphasizing benevolence, tolerance, camaraderie, brotherhood.

The great difficulty with humanitarianism, as many people use the word and the idea, is that it represents an unanchored concept adrift in foggy space. It has slipped its moorings. For a theory which announces the brotherhood of man implies some sort of fatherhood. Only because they have a common father are men called brothers. Divorced from the fatherhood of God, "from whom all fatherhood in heaven and on earth receives its name" (Eph. 3:15), the brotherhood of man becomes merely a nominal fraternity with no real background of causality, no solid lineage. We are, therefore, concentrating on the less important aspect of a compound idea if we fix on *human*itarianism and forget what, for the sake of balance, we might call *divin*itarianism; if we look only at man, and ignore God.

The Sunday within the Octave of the Ascension recalls these truths to us as it reminds us of the wondrous day, centuries ago, when, before the adoring gaze of His disciples, Christ "was lifted up . . . and a cloud took him out of their sight" (Acts 1:9). In Him were the two complete natures, the divine and the human, now immeasurably dignified because it had been assumed by the Eternal Word, who, as Augustine points out, "carried up our humanity into the heights above"; to so lofty a seat, Chrysostom adds, that man "could ascend no higher."

Because of this union of human with divine nature, man is holy. Consequently, man deserves not only the cold offices of tolerance, which John Lothrop Motley says is "a phrase of insult," but is worthy of the warmest esteem, the supernatural benevolence which is charity. "All flesh was sanctified," as Father McGucken wrote, ". . . since the day that the Word was made flesh and dwelt amongst us." That is the real basis of genuine humanism and humanitarianism. That is the dogmatic background of Saint Peter's exhortation in the epistle of today's Mass: "But above all things have a constant mutual charity among

yourselves . . . be hospitable to one another without mur-
muring." That is the lovely union Saint John mentions:
"Our fellowship . . . with the Father, and with his Son,
Jesus Christ" (1 John 1:3).

The fact that we are, by grace, the adopted children
of God, the brothers and sisters of Jesus, is one of those
convictions which, if reduced to the order of "living ideas,"
could change the world. Charitableness then would not be
merely a sentimental philanthropy inspired by Christmas
music or a crippled child, but a daily, tireless attitude embracing all men. Only by the grace of God can man attain
such an outlook.

Writing over a hundred years ago, Guizot, the historian
of civilization, exulted that "the age of barbaric Europe
with its brute force, its violence, its lies and deceit" had
passed, that the time had come when "man's condition
shall be progressively improved by the force of reason and
truth." He staked out his earthly paradise somewhat pre-
maturely. But the time now is when truth could improve
man's condition, the transforming truth of man's incorporation in Christ and the corollaries deriving from that incorporation. These corollaries have been shiningly stated by
Father Mersch: "To forget oneself, to renounce oneself,
in order to belong to Christ, to God and to every man,
that is the spectacle that will make manifest to all, in the
manner that will strike them, *that Christ still lives in His
own.*"

Filled with the Holy Spirit

Acts 2:4

Pentecost is a day resonant with elemental forces: the mighty wind shaking Jerulasem; eloquent fire above the Apostles; earth renewed by the Spirit's visitation (Ps. 103:30) and water touched to sacramental power so that of it and the Holy Spirit man might henceforward be reborn to supernatural life (John 3:5).

It is a feast of hope, assurance, strength and transformation, as the change in Christ's disciples attests. Puzzled by prophecies of the resurrection (Mark 9:9), they had scoffed at reports of fulfillment, shrugging them off as "nonsense" (Luke 24:11). "Foolish and slow of heart to believe" (Luke 24:25), they thought the risen Christ was a phantom. Thomas disgracefully demanded proof before he would assent (John 20:25) and Our Lord upbraided all of them for their incredulity (Mark 16:14). Even at the ascension there were lingering doubts (Matt. 28:17) and apparent misapprehensions about the kingdom Jesus would establish (Acts 1:6).

Truly they were not a promising little phalanx to be entrusted with the conversion of the world. But their Master had assured them He would not abandon them in their helplessness (John 14:18). He had reassured them on Ascension Day: "you shall be baptized with the Holy Spirit not many days hence" (Acts 1:5), by which He signified not the sacrament of baptism but a further, full outpouring of the Spirit. The wind which roared through Jerusalem on Pentecost was an outward sign of that power which transmuted these vainglorious, timorous men into the valorous messengers of God whose "voice," as Paul, quoting Psalm 18, writes, "has gone forth into all the earth and their words unto the ends of the world" (Rom. 10:18).

Centuries before, David with a handful of warriors and a faltering heart had faced the overwhelming host of the Philistines. He called on God, who commanded a flanking movement instead of a frontal assault, for He ordered David to deploy his thin troops near a pear orchard. "And when thou shalt hear the sound of one going in the tops of the pear trees, then shalt thou join battle: for then will the Lord go out before thy face to strike the army of the Philistines" (2 Kings 5:24). David obeyed and when a thrashing torrent of sound lashed the tree-tops, the Israelites charged and hurled back the foe, reeling and broken. The Pentecostal wind indicated the presence of the same divine power by which the apostles went out and conquered the world. "I am with you all days" was the divine promise and they "were sealed with the Holy Spirit of the promise" (Eph. 1:13).

Seldom is the Spirit manifested externally, as it was on the first Pentecost. The whirling wind has softened to the constant susurrus of grace in the individual soul. Yet no less definitely than the apostles did we receive the Holy Spirit in baptism. We have our personal Pentecost in the sacrament of confirmation. We have its frequent renewal in the other sacraments and the daily inspirations of grace within us, calling us to personal holiness and to the Christian career of apostolic example which would influence other men. The Holy Spirit has the power to transform us as He transformed the apostles. The memorable conversion of Saint Mary Magdalen shall always remind us that He who could stun a city can certainly awaken a human heart from its sinful stupor. But He is no divine marauder forcing His way into our souls. He summons, inspires, invites. He does not violate our liberty.

The trouble, obviously, is with us, blinded as we are by worldliness and sensuality and falling under the penalty described by Paul: "The sensual man does not perceive the things that are of the Spirit of God" (I Cor. 2:14). Paul cries out on us to harken to the Spirit, to heed His inspirations. "Do not extinguish the Spirit," he begs (1 Thess. 5:20) and again, "do not grieve the Holy Spirit of God" (Eph. 4:30).

From Him . . . Through Him . . . Unto Him . . .

Romans 11:36

Reverence is an idea which the contemporary mind too often dismisses as a mildewed survival of medievalism. It is considered akin to servility, a bar to proper self-expression, understandable enough in a serf twisting his peasant forelock before his suzerain, but utterly unworthy of a democratic citizen. This attitude translates itself into a general lack of respect for law and authority, into the flippancy of the young towards parent or preceptor, into the casualness of man to woman.

There is a whole school of journalism and literature whose mentality was once accurately described as "calculated irreverence." Nothing to them is sacred, nothing outside the reach of satire. Anything like reverence is stabbed with a gibe or impaled on an epithet, called "quaint," "old-world" or simply "corny." Men like John Galsworthy, adept at the urbane sneer, and H. G. Wells, more boisterously blasphemous, did not spare even God. May He rest them both.

Trinity Sunday, however, has reverence as its keynote. In its fullest realization, this reverence is a blend of those two gifts of the Holy Spirit, piety and fear. Piety un-fortunately is a word which popular misuse has badly battered. In its real meaning, it denotes adoration com-bined with abandonment to God's holy will, but warmed by filial love and confidence in the Heavenly Father. It is perfect trust which never lapses into presumption, freedom which never degenerates into familiarity. It lovingly recalls God's mercy while not forgetting His majesty and His justice.

Complementary to piety is that "holy fear" (Ps. 18:10) which, not at all irreconcilable with joy (Ps. 2:11), "is all wisdom" (Ecclus. 19:18) and, in fact, "the beginning of love" (Ecclus. 25:16). Even the angels before the throne of God have this blessed fear, as the Common Preface reminds us. Saint Paul exhorts us to the same: "We have grace, through which we may offer pleasing service to God with fear and reverence. For our God is a consuming fire" (Heb. 12:28).

Likewise in the epistle of the Trinity Sunday Mass, in tones muted with awe, the apostle exclaims: "Oh, the depth of the riches of the wisdom and the knowledge of God! How incomprehensible are his judgments and how unsearchable his ways!" It is a reprimand to us who quarrel with the divine designs because they disappoint us, a re-buke to our rebelliousness, a warning to bend our stiff

necks and knees before Him to whom Saint Teresa custom-
arily referred simply as "His Majesty."

The feast of Corpus Christi, which occurs this week,
reinforces the point. The Mass and Office, composed by
Aquinas, are hushed with adoration, prostrate dependence,
profound love. Saint Paul's epistle warns us of the dreadful
crime of receiving the Blessed Sacrament unworthily, becoming thereby "guilty of the Body and Blood of the Lord"
(1 Cor. 11:28). The Communion prayer repeats the theme.

The official prayers of the Church delineate the proper
reverence with which we should approach the sacred mysteries. As the priest enters the sacristy, he washes his hands
and begs the grace of absolute purity of body and mind.
As he vests, he continues the petition. At the foot of the
altar, he pleads for deliverance "from the nation that is
not holy" and "the unjust and deceitful man" before he
bows to make confession of his sins. As he passes over to
read the gospel, he again asks God to purify him. Those
alert Catholics who are active participants in the sacrifice
make these prayers their own.

Unfortunately, however, there are many who are merely
passive spectators at the renewal of Calvary. They have not
piety: that great virtue of adoration, filial love and confidence felt in God's Presence. They lack "holy fear"—
the counterpart of piety—reverent fear that enriches man's
love of God in the service of God. They pay no heed to the
presence of God in their lives. They seldom partake fully
of the Holy Sacrifice, seldom receive Holy Communion.
Reverence for God is what they need and reverence for
God is what they lack—reverence for God, the Father who
created them; God, the Son who redeemed them; God the
Holy Ghost who confirmed them.

And today—Trinity Sunday—the priest leaves the altar of sacrifice and enters the pulpit to proclaim this message of mercy: "All things are from Him," God, the Father; "All things are through Him," God, the Son; "All things are unto Him," God, the Holy Ghost, the Sanctifier. This is the message that moves us, all of us who have been faithful, to greater love and deeper gratitude; this is the message that invites those who have been prodigal sons to return to the banquet table, the altar of plenty, spread by a bountiful God.

We Have Come to Know His Love

1 John 3:16

Jehu, an Old Testament king, rudely dethroned by modern dictionaries and made the humorous patron of reckless driving, was the valiant leader whose chariot wheels and voice of command resound through the Fourth Book of Kings. One day Jehu encountered Jonadab, son of Rechab, and asked him a question which touches the very essence of loyalty: "Is thy heart right," he said, "as my heart is with thy heart?" (4 Kings 10:15). June, the month of the Sacred Heart, "king and center of all hearts," might very well recall that query to us. In our secret souls we might well imagine One—of whom Jehu's very name reminds us—asking that same searching question of each of us: "Is thy heart right, as My Heart is with thy heart?"

Significantly enough, the epistles for the first Sunday after Pentecost and the Sunday within the octave of Corpus Christi, are both drawn from the First Epistle of Saint John, the disciple of love. They are epistles of the heart, moving and beautiful. "God is love," says the apostle. "In this was the love of God shown in our case, that God has sent his only-begotten Son into the world that we may live through him" (I John 4:8, 9). And again, in the Mass for the Sunday within the octave of Corpus Christi, the theme recurs. We prove our love for God by our love of our brethren. "He who has the goods of this world and sees his brother in need and closes his heart to him, how does the love of God abide in him?" (1 John 3:17).

Likewise in the epistle for the Feast of the Sacred Heart, which falls within this week, Saint Paul proclaims "the good tidings of the unfathomable riches of Christ" and prays the Father to grant that his disciples may be strengthened and "have Christ dwelling through faith in your hearts" (Eph. 3:9, 17). These epistles all show a remarkably unified liturgical and theological motif, revealing to us the Heart of Christ, as once He disclosed it to Margaret Mary: inexhaustibly rich, immemorially loving, yet repaid, for the most part, by coldness, indifference, ingratitude in our hearts, which certainly are not "right with His Heart."

The heart in history most closely conforming to His was, of course, the Immaculate Heart of Mary, which we venerated in the month just past. Her Divine Son privately revealed to Saint Mechtilde how perfectly Mary's heart mirrored His own, and He instructed the saint to salute Our Lady's Heart, "as the most pure heart that has ever existed except My own." And again, "This admirable mother bore Me lovingly in her heart before she conceived

Me in her womb," that is, she perfectly realized in her life the ideals which He came to establish and exemplify, as Saint Leo notes in one of his sermons. One cannot separate the hearts of Jesus and Mary, as Saint John Eudes declares. To meditate on the one is to think of the other. And there is no better path to the Heart of Jesus, as the same saint asserts, than through the heart of Mary.

At the time when Christ revealed His Heart to men, human reason, exalted beyond its large but limited scope, was on a pedestal, crowned and canonized. The divine answer to the haughty mind of man was the humble Heart of God. In our day, too, and in our individual souls, pride, self-sufficiency and boastful rationalism have prominent place. We have not learned the bitter lessons which current history thrusts upon us. Though man, who would not kneel in humility, has twice in a quarter-century been beaten to his knees by the sheer weight of adversity, he has not particularly profited. Reform, as Pius XII has told us, must take place not only in council and code but more basically in each human heart.

But do not content yourself with agreeing to abstract generalities. You have a heart of your own; for it you are alone responsible. How do you answer the question, asked now not by Jehu but Jesus: "Is thy heart right as My heart is, with thy heart?"

Humble Yourself

I Peter 5:6

From the way many Catholics talk and—more important—act, one might get the impression that humility had taken the veil and retired exclusively to the convent; that humility is a concern of cowl and cloister but has no place outside the consecrated garth; that it is a charming trait in nuns, most becoming to monks, but a flaw allied to servility or cowardice in a man of the world. That Saint Peter, the first infallible custodian of truth, did not agree to this attitude is crushingly clear from the section of his first epistle read in the Mass for the third Sunday after Pentecost.

"Humble yourself under the mighty hand of God," he writes, "that he may exalt you in the time of visitation."

Years before, Peter, then unformed and spiritually illiterate, had heard His Master declare: "For everyone who exalts himself shall be humbled, and he who humbles himself shall be exalted" (Luke 14:11). He had learned the lesson well. In this very letter, his preceding sentence had been: "God resists the proud, but gives grace to the humble"; and Saint James insists on the same high and hard truth: "Humble yourselves in the Lord and he will exalt you" (James 4:10).

The idea that God humbled those who presumed on their own strength was an ancient one among the Jews (Judith 6:15). "There is one that humbleth and exalteth, God who seeth all," says the book of Ecclesiasticus (7:12). But Jesus had revived and reinvigorated the notion, setting it out in unforgettable clarity through His passion and death. Perhaps the highest expression of the ideal was the swelling hymn which burst from the most pure heart of a young girl, espoused by the Holy Spirit, who spoke through her lips, "My soul magnifies the Lord . . . Because He has regarded the lowliness of His handmaid . . . He has shown might with His arm, He has scattered the proud in the conceit of their heart. He has put down the mighty from their thrones, and has exalted the lowly" (Luke 1:46, 52).

Now humility is a chastening or restraining virtue which keeps man's warring inclinations in gyroscopic equipoise. It holds the middle place between pride, which is not Christian but satanic, and obsequiousness, which is not Christian but contemptible. It consists, says Thomas Aquinas, "in keeping oneself within one's own bounds, not reaching out to things above one but submitting to one's superior." Let us imagine, for a moment, by way of indulging man's insatiable longing for Utopia, a world in which all men were humble in the sense delineated by Aquinas.

It would be a world in which each man estimated himself properly, appreciating his true talents and thanking God for them, appraising accurately his real limitations and accepting them resignedly. Each man would live within the budget of what he actually had; and sham, pretension and hypocrisy would be on their way into exile. Conscious of his own defects, a man would be less likely to concentrate uncharitably on those of his neighbor, which would notably reduce unkind talk, jealousy and envy. In other words, the superlative of "good" would once again be elevated, grammatically and ideologically, to the position of aloof uniqueness which it justly deserves; because each of us would stop thinking that he was the best, the high-mark of human striving, the man whom the sweating centuries had conspired to produce.

A humble world would be a lovely world, to be sure. That was the world, as the Scriptures tell us, which God intended and man, urged by his "adversary the devil," revised. But once again, it is easy and impersonal and un-embarrassing to talk about "the world." How about that microcosm, your own mind, your own heart? Are they humble, filled with the Petrine conviction that only Christ can "perfect, strengthen and establish us"?

Dwelling by Faith in Your Hearts

Ephesians 3:17

Devotions in the Church are not sudden flares of sentiment or impulse or feeling. They are solid growths which mature slowly from deep and unshakable roots of dogma. Catholicism does not rest content in the sterile contemplation of truth nor in Euclidean glimpses of beauty bare. The profound and eternal truth of dogma flowers into devotion, into acts of reverence and love and service. And so, abiding beneath the shrines and the litanies, acts of consecration and all the other phases of the Sacred Heart devotion, there are soul-shattering doctrines.

One bleak morning, long ago in Bethlehem, Mary held on her breast Jesus Christ, who was her Son and the Son of God. Her baby was an intensely human child, with a human nature like unto our own, as Saint Paul points out, in everything save sin. Yet at the same time, her baby was God, having as His own by right of eternal generation from His Eternal Father, the divine nature.

Here there is no room for metaphor or loose talk. Ages ago, Arius wanted to explain away the divine sonship as a position of princely precedence in all creation. Hence, the Son of God could be so called only in the sense that He was the first-born masterpiece of God's creative power; the recipient, to an incredible degree, of God's grace and favor. But in no other sense.

Nestorius, looking at the child on Mary's bosom, saw in Him two distinct persons; one human, the son of the Virgin; the other, divine, the Son of God. Between these two persons there existed a most intimate union, for the Divine Word indwelt in the human Christ. But the union was merely moral; and Mary, the mother of Christ the Man, was not the mother of God.

In his anti-Nestorian zeal, Eutyches likewise erred. Even after the Incarnation, he declared, there was still only one nature in Christ; and the followers of Eutyches fell into various theological camps according as they explained the union of divine and human natures as absorption of the human by the divine or a fusion of both natures into one.

With the passing of time, these heresies crumpled and collapsed before the volleys of such champions as Athanasius, Cyril of Alexandria and Leo the Great and beneath the condemnations of the Councils. From the controversies and definitions, there emerges a clear, dogmatic description of the God-man and it is on this that the devotion to the Sacred Heart ultimately and solidly rests.

In Our Lord there are two natures, whole and complete,

the divine and the human. These natures are mysteriously united in the One Person, Jesus Christ, who, consequently, is to be adored with the highest and most sublime worship, which we are forbidden to render to any mere creature, even Our Lady—the adoration which belongs only to God. When we adore God, we prostrate ourselves in submissive recognition of and testimony to His infinite and ineffable excellence. It is easy to see that we must pay this complete homage to Our Lord insofar as He is divine. But the further question arises: What about Christ as a man? He has also an integral human nature. May or rather must we also adore His humanity?

Before answering that question, the Church makes the issue perfectly clear. The sacred humanity is a creature and as such cannot be adored for its own sake. But the Word of God, Second Person of the Most Blessed Trinity, assumed that humanity, which is, therefore, as Athanasius writes, "the body of God". Hence it is adorable because it is the human body of a Divine Person; and while the act of adoration is directed to the sacred body of Christ or to its several members, the reason and motive of the worship is the limitless perfection of the Divine Person whose sacred body this is.

That is the theological background for the adoration of the Sacred Heart of Jesus. Although the devotion was occasioned by the private revelation to Saint Margaret Mary, we must not identify the devotion and the revelation. For the real force and dogmatic validity of the apparition derives from the approbation of the teaching Church, to whom alone it pertains to speak definitively and finally on faith and morals.

All down the years, the Church had adored the sacred

humanity which the Word of God assumed. And in that
sacred body, the Heart of flesh is a prominent organ. But
we must not think of that Heart as a withered relic. It is
the living, breathing, pulsing Heart, alive with eternal
vitality and still united to the Second Person of the Blessed
Trinity. In the natural heraldry of all peoples, moreover, the
heart has a symbolic significance which is readily recognized. Everyday experience teaches us that it races, con-
tracts, palpitates or hangs like a stone within us at times
of great emotional upheaval. Whatever the psychological
explanation of this may be, the heart has come to be a
symbol of man's inner sentiments, especially his love.

So, too, with the Heart of Christ. We look on it as the
symbol of all of Christ's inner sentiments, especially His
great love for His Father and for men. Glowing in that
Heart is the gash of the spear, as Saint Bonaventure tells
us, in order that, beholding the visible wound, we might
see the invisible wound of love. That burning and broken
Heart, then, is a call to love and to reparation for the cold
indifference with which men have repaid Christ's infinite
kindness to them. Consecration and expiation are the acts
of worship which Our Lord has explicitly requested. "Consecration," as Pope Pius XI wrote, "by which we offer to
the Divine Heart of Jesus both ourselves and all that belongs to us." But, as the same venerable authority goes on
to show, a desire to atone for the outrages heaped upon
the Sacred Heart is a natural and complementary outgrowth of sincere consecration.

Our Lord, of course, is far beyond the reach of pain
or sorrow; nevermore will they touch Him. But there was
that black night under the olive trees when He staggered
and fell beneath the weight of the world's iniquities, when

He lay with His face in the damp loam of Gethsemane and His flesh shriveled and crawled with the horrible anticipation of the sufferings to come. That night His Sacred Heart was beating so furiously and wildly that It forced His blood out through His pores. And the vision which tormented Him included the crowds, and the trials and the scourges and the cross. But with a far greater intensity, that scalding vision comprised the long generations of men who would not benefit by His sufferings or repay His sacrifices with anything but ingratitude. Still, while He foresaw the crimes of men and flinched at the vision, He was solaced in that bitter hour by His foreknowledge of faithful souls who would assume the burden of atonement. He was solaced by the shining company of the saints, both those canonized on the altars and in anonymity, by the bright battalions that march through the *Te Deum*—the confessors, virgins, martyrs.

To assume the burden of reparation, therefore, is what the devotion to the Sacred Heart calls on us to do. It is a call which no generous heart can disregard. When, in the seventeenth century, the drab light of reason was already graying the world, when passing time had chilled man's memory of Calvary and formed the ice of Jansenism on man's heart; then Christ made this burning revelation of His love to a humble nun in Burgundy. He commissioned her to arouse an indifferent world to flaming love. The story of the diffusion of that appeal against odds which seemed insuperable is another stirring chapter in the conquest of the wise by the simple and the foolish.

Out from the quiet of Paray-le-Monial that call and message reverberated through all Christendom. It was in the very year in which Spinoza was writing to the young and imprudently zealous Catholic convert, Albert Brugh, a blasphemous sneer at one who believed "that you swallow the highest and the eternal." There was a heavenly paradox in the fact that during the age which enthroned in untouchable sovereignty the mind of man, devotion to the Heart of God was spreading with a rapidity that the Church calls "triumphant."

Today that message and devotion are still vital, still dynamic. The Sacred Heart is our real sign and assurance. Long centuries ago, before Our Lord came on earth, as Pius XI declares, God made a covenant of friendship with man. As a seal of that covenant, He flung a gleaming arc across the sky, "a bow appearing in the clouds." Ages later, as Leo XIII remarks and Pius XI recalls, a young Roman Emperor was preparing for battle; and the yoke lay heavy on Christ's infant Church. One night a cross burned high in the heavens as a sign and a seal of complete victory.

With these historic manifestations of God's relations with men, the Pontiffs link up that most auspicious and gracious sign of our times . . . "the most Sacred Heart of Jesus, crested with a cross, gleaming amid incandescent flames. In this sign we must place all our hopes . . ." These Fathers of universal Christendom ardently desired that Christ should be the King of all hearts, the King of all hearths. The home in which the Sacred Heart is enthroned and honored has the divine guarantee of blessings. For Christ promised: "I will give peace to their families. I will bless the houses wherein the image of my Sacred Heart will be exposed and honored."

In his Epistle to the Ephesians, Saint Paul in a few, swift strokes, outlined the lineaments of the true Christian home. With divinely supported authority, he sketched the relationships of husband and wife and children to parents. Writing to Father Matheo, one of the great apostles of the enthronement of the Sacred Heart, Cardinal Billot recalled Paul's descriptions and asked: "What think you, Reverend Father? Is not this a description of the interior of a household where the Sacred Heart would be enthroned?"

This holy dedication of the individual and the family to the Sacred Heart is no mere passing pietism nor emotional whim, as Benedict XV solemnly declares. That great Pontiff insisted that consecration which does not fructify in daily virtues is sterile and meaningless. "Faith, charity, zeal in prayer, temperance, domestic tranquility"—these are the living proofs of a vital and fruitful consecration. "The old should find strength, the young prudence, the afflicted comfort, the infirm patience, in the Sacred Heart of Jesus."

That was the splendid assurance of Christ's Vicar to an exhausted and panting world, seven months after the first world war had ended. We should ponder those words now and explore their possibilities for our own day, even more woebegone than that in which the Pope first spoke. Still does the Sacred Heart call for love, for consecration, for reparation: still do His promises obtain. Today and during the rose-reddened month of June, all over the world rise hymns of praise and adoration to the Heart which wrought our salvation. Quietly and unspectacularly, devotion to the Sacred Heart has suffused the world with warmth, and has given the lie to Swinburne's shocking apostrophe to the "pale Galilean."

Suffering Compared to the Glory to Come

Romans 8:18

Human hope is a flame, a flag, an enticing fragrance; it is the lamp and hearth at the end of a black road; it is the outboard motor which keeps thousands of mortal derelicts chugging along, no matter how high the combers, deep the troughs. It is the only medicine of the miserable, said Shakespeare; it springs eternal, added Pope; and many a Micawber, aimless but dauntless, has gladdened the heart of the world with his undismayed and jaunty *"Nil desperandum"*—never give up hope!

But the hope which animates the epistle for the fourth Sunday after Pentecost is not merely man's natural and recurrent optimism, his resilient ingenuity in salvaging shattered causes or converting hideous wounds into honorable scars. Paul speaks of theological or divine hope, as it is called because of its origin and its object; and such hope is a gift of God, totally undeserved by man. It floods the soul, along with faith and love, when God in His goodness lifts us to a supernatural state to which by our own strength we could neither aspire nor attain.

Divine hope is called a habit, but we do not here mean by habit an acquired facility, an established pattern of action achieved through repeated practice. Habit, in this sense, signifies a faculty of operation, a stable power of performance, the result of God's generosity rather than man's endeavor. Supernatural hope does not merely strengthen or perfect a natural aptitude; it sublimates, transforms and elevates it to a supernatural efficiency at which, unaided, it could never arrive.

The relation of hope to the other divinely bestowed habits of faith and love, Saint Thomas indicates when he writes: these are "faith, by which we know God; hope, by which we trust to attain Him; and charity, by which we love Him." We should pray constantly for a growth of "these three" in our souls as the Church insists in her prayer: "Give unto us, O Lord, increase of faith, hope and charity."

The Romans to whom Paul was writing were no strangers to sorrow in that decadent city which Tacitus, not many years later, was to describe as the central, seething sewer of the world. About that same time, Pliny would be asking Trajan "whether the mere profession of Christianity, albeit without any criminal act [was to be considered a violation of the law]; or are only the crimes associated therewith punishable." The handwriting was on the wall, with enemies without, tensions and factions within the Christian community.

Yet all the sufferings of the present, Paul assures them, are a small price to pay for the blinding "glory to come that will be revealed in us." The union with Christ and possession of the Holy Spirit in life will explode into full, final radiance after this life.

Each of us in these days of doubt should brand this invigorating conviction into his consciousness, that the only worthy object of one's hope is "the God of my heart, and the God that is my portion forever." For it is good "to put my hope in the Lord God" (Ps. 72:26, 28). The disciples on the road to Emmaus were the classic example of men unhappy because their hopes were not conformed to the divine plan. "They were hoping that it was He who should redeem Israel" (Luke 24:13) but their ideas were at variance with God's idea, and Christ called them "foolish ones and slow of heart." Those disciples founded a club which still has a large membership.

Quite otherwise was Paul's prayer: "Blessed be the God and Father of Our Lord Jesus Christ, the Father of mercies and the God of all comfort, who comforts us in all our afflictions" (2 Cor. 1:3). That was the way the saints prayed. Xavier, dying, cried out: "In thee, O Lord, have I hoped, let me never be confounded" (Ps. 31:1). It is a good prayer, living and dying.

Who Is There to Harm You?

1 Peter 3:13

The matter of human relations has, in our day, been elevated practically to the status of a science, complete with theories, experts and developed techniques. Big business employs psychiatrists to unravel those temperamental tangles which may reduce a worker's efficiency. Intricate explorations of aptitude and psychological stability are routine. Over the radio people air their intimate troubles before a panel of advisers. The science of gaining friends—which, in the benighted past was a simple affair of emotional impulse and common interests—has been reduced to foolproof equations in a best-seller. Hostesses and receptionists are technically trained for the involved vocation of meeting their fellowmen suavely and successfully. Personal charm has been distilled in psychosomatic laboratories and made a commodity to be bought in a bottle or culled from a book. Yet, with all this, we are faced with the paradoxical and disagreeable fact that our times have witnessed the most tragic collapse of human relationships which the world has ever seen. The international world, when not openly at war, is tense with glowering suspicion. The papers are full of divorce, murder, violence and lawlessness. And even that mild and amiable "average citizen" we talk about is, in traffic, store or subway, not always recognizably a graduate of a school of charm. Perhaps the fact that Alphonse and Gaston are strictly comic characters may be, if you think it out, more of a damning commentary on our civilization than you would at first suspect.

In the passage from Saint Peter's first epistle, read in the Mass for the fifth Sunday after Pentecost, the first Pope continues to sketch for his struggling flock the ideal Christian. It is well to remind ourselves that God is the principal, and Peter only the secondary or instrumental author of the portrait. The characterization is therefore not merely an idealization to be admired but an actual goal which, with God's help, we must achieve. And so few of us really resemble the model that we can scarcely wonder at the chaotic state of society and our own souls.

Take up the elements of characters which Peter lists. The Christian must be united to his fellows, compassionate, merciful, reserved (or modest), humble, "not rendering evil for evil . . . but contrariwise, blessing," honest and zealous for what is good. Natural virtue alone cannot produce a man with those endowments. The civilized smile of natural virtue too easily curls into a snarl.

The compassion Peter speaks about is not a disdainful

philanthropic dole, but a deep charity of the heart. James
Russell Lowell's Sir Launfal, immaculately mailed, splendidly mounted, shining in young strength, rearing back his
horse in revulsion at the sight of a beggar and then tossing
him a pittance, is not the symbol of real sympathy, mercy
or compassion. Contrast with him the young Francis of
Assisi, stricken with remorse and returning to kiss the
verminous vagrant he had spurned; or Martin of Tours
sharing his cloak with a shivering stranger. Both of them
in *fact*, as Launfal in *fiction*, found Christ and the Grail
not in distant lands or great enterprises but in their neighbor; and in their souls sounded a quiet voice: "As long as
you did it for one of these, the least of my brethren, you
did it for me" (Matt. 25:45).

List, some time, the qualities which are the outstanding
characteristics of your own soul and then compare your
self-description with the portrait of the Christian which
Saint Peter outlines in his epistle. The autobiographical
analysis would reveal all too many of us as compassionate
only in fits and starts, under impulse of sentimentality
rather than sanctity. We would discover that we are not
merciful but vindictive, swift to resent, slow to retract,
prone to render evil for evil. And a world or a home or a
human heart in which such vices reside cannot but be an
uneasy battleground.

Baptized into His Death

Romans 6:3

So candent, complete and compelling was Saint Paul's love of Jesus Christ that he could compress his whole career into an epigram and submerge his selfhood in a holy anonymity. "For to me," he wrote, "to live is Christ and to die is gain" (Phil. 1:21); and, again, "It is now no longer I that live, but Christ lives in me" (Gal. 2:20).

Paul was a highly educated man, tutored at home by his Pharisaic father (Acts 23:6) and later a student under the great Gamaliel himself (Acts 22:3). Yet, despite the richness and range of his mind, the subtlety of his doctrine and his stylistic mastery, he considered all learning unimportant compared with the "excellent knowledge" of his Lord: "For I determined not to know anything among

you, except Jesus Christ and him crucified" (1 Cor. 2:2).
Absolutely nothing else mattered to this blazing and dedicated spirit: "For his sake I have suffered the loss of all
things, and I count them as dung that I may gain Christ"
(Phil. 3:8). Apostolic agony, which he compared to travail,
racked him as he labored to bring other men to a knowledge
and love of his Master; he was anxious to spend "and be
spent myself for your souls," as he told the Corinthians
(2 Cor. 12:15).

The epistle of the Mass for the sixth Sunday after
Pentecost finds Paul still hammering home the central
thesis of his preaching: that the union between Christ and
the Christian is incredibly intimate, that the life of the
Christian is a continuation of the life of Christ. "All we
who have been baptized into Christ Jesus," he writes,
"have been baptized into his death." Father Prat, the
great Pauline scholar, explaining this baptism "into Christ,"
says that thereby we are not merely subjected to Him
as slaves to a master or liegemen to a lord, not just bound
to Him in fealty or consecrated to Him as an edifice might
be to a divinity. "It is still more and above all to be incorporated with Him, to be immersed in Him, as if in a new
element, to become a part of Him as another self."

Hence after baptism we have everything in common
with Our Lord. We share with Him His crucifixion, burial,
resurrection, His new life, glorious reign and ineffable
heritage. So close is the union, so living the link, that Paul
elsewhere expresses it by the figure of a branch engrafted
on a vital trunk and absorbed, assimilated, nourished by
the life of the foster-parental tree (Rom. 11:17).

The impact and implications of this stunning truth can
be explored and appreciated, under grace, only in prayer,

the best medium, as Blessed Claude de la Colombière intimates, for transmuting theology into spirituality. But one obvious conclusion is that if we have any sense of fitness, any consistency, we must try to resemble the Incarnate Word in His actions no less than in His dispositions of soul.

Go back to the life of Christ. See it begin in the precious womb of Our Lady, coming to the light in wintry Bethlehem, blossoming in the exile of Egypt, flowering in the humble obscurity of Nazareth under Mary's adoring eyes and Joseph's smile, reaching full stature in the teaching years, declining at the scourging pillar, snuffed out on the cross. Look at His Heart as He revealed it to us—meek, humble, obedient, perfectly alert and amenable to the Father's will, infinitely compassionate, scorning only hypocrisy. He is our Head; we are His members.

Now look at your own life, your actions, your consistent dispositions of soul. Can you wonder that in a latter-day revelation of His Heart Jesus sadly pointed out the contrast between His Heart, which loved men so much, and man's heart, usually ungrateful, indifferent, cold?

The Wages of Sin Is Death

Romans 6:23

Life has often been imaged as a house or mansion in which the various rooms represent man's departmentalized interests. Into one room he goes to work, into another to play, into a third to eat; and so each phase of his existence is symbolized. But it is a dangerous mistake to assign one room in that mansion to religion, thereby making the worship and love of God just one more concern of man, on a par with the rest. In the castle of life, religion is the foundation, the strength permeating each beam and stay. It is the walls, giving cohesion, unity and totality to disparate elements, enveloping and ennobling all within. It is the roof over all, protective and pointed towards God. Religion is an all-inclusive force, infiltrating and interpenetrating all of life's actions, motivating them properly, orienting them towards their First Cause and Final End.

The Catholic who makes his faith just another of his interests, extracurricular to the main course of life, is in a fatal state spiritually. Unfortunately there are many such. They are supernaturally drowsy. Their minds are listless; their wills limp. They fear thoroughness, which they conveniently term fanaticism. They will not wet their cautious feet in the rushing Rubicons of religion. They are too short-winded for mountain-climbing in any spiritual Darien. With them, faith is a series of unrelated interludes, not a coherent career. And Saint Paul, for all of his broad sympathy, seems to have found it extremely difficult to understand them. He was uncomprisingly a Catholic. He was desperately apostolic, hoarse from persuading his disciples to make certain of the "one thing necessary." A man who had received the faith, assented to the doctrine and then failed to think through its derivatives and meet its demands was to Paul spiritually demented.

In the epistle for the seventh Sunday after Pentecost, Paul is working along the lines of that inexorable logic. Before your conversion, he tells the Romans, you were "slaves of uncleanness," dedicated to debauchery, seeking happiness in unrestrained license. Now you are regenerated, born again of water and the Holy Spirit, indentured to God. As in your days of abandon you gave yourselves completely to the quest of carnal happiness, so now with corresponding generosity you should hunger and thirst after justice, seeking God and real happiness.

This section of his letter to the Romans occurs soon after the passage read in last Sunday's Mass, in which Paul had insisted so strongly on their union with Christ. Now

he expounds the imperative necessity of following out the
consequences of that union, a necessity which his Divine
Master had previously expressed in the dichotomy: "No
man can serve two masters; for either he will hate the one
and love the other, or he will be loyal to one and despise
the other. You cannot serve God and mammon" (Luke
16:13). And even more strongly: "He who is not with me
is against me, and he who does not gather with me scatters"
(Matt. 12:30). Christ rejects casual love and parenthetical
service with frightening finality. So, too, does Paul.

We who are the children of light can readily lapse into
a minor Pharisaism. We can grant religion its stuffy little
closet in our house of life and spend our few grudging
minutes there each day or week. Meantime, we reserve
the "right" to retain principles which flatly contradict our
labial profession of faith, and leave "undone the weightier
matters of the law, right judgment and mercy and faith"
(Matt. 23:23). Of what avail is it to light a vigil candle
and shortly thereafter extinguish a reputation? Is it not
self-deception to be a liar, a snob, unjust to employer or
employe, obese of soul generally, and still to think oneself
a Catholic because one goes to Sunday Mass?

Catholicism is not merely a creed of lip; it is also a
culture and a full-time career. Catholicism is not the practice of going to church on Sunday casually but of looking
at the whole of life or rather life as a whole. A genuinely
real Catholic, a loyal follower of Christ, has acquired the
habit of looking at all his activities and of spontaneously
correlating the practice of churchgoing with the motives
which color all his dealings, all his transactions all days of
the week. There is no day of the week when Catholicism

takes a holiday; every day for the real Catholic is a holy day, a sacred day, a day consecrated to Christ who taught: "No man can serve two masters"—"you cannot serve God and mammon."

Joint Heirs with Christ

Romans 8:17

American magazines, as mirrors of American morality and mentality, might persuade that handy, hypothetical visitor from Mars that we are a race of body-worshipers. Page after page pictures ultra-sophisticated ladies, irresistibly perfumed, and intent—if one accepts the implication of the captions—on seduction. Our marriages, the Martian might conclude, are founded not on a community of basic interest but on a civility of charm, hair-do, and make-up. Suitable lotions are more important than right emotions; scent is of greater moment than soul. Daring has replaced decency as the designer of bathing-suit and gown; the sun has re-emerged as a god in the cult of tan-charmers. Story, advertisement and illustration conspire to reject the phrase which is the title of one of Evelyn Waugh's books, *Vile Bodies;* and literature increasingly portrays man as merely a highly organized system of antennae, a receiving set for sensations.

In the epistle for the eighth Sunday after Pentecost, Saint Paul, writing to the Romans, who also apotheosized the body, strikes out against this canonization of the carnal: "for if you live according to the flesh you will die; but if by the spirit you put to death the deeds of the flesh, you will live." There Paul indicates the two hostile factions which make human life a warfare on earth; the "law in my members," which he had mentioned in the previous chapter, "warring against the law of my mind," against "the law of God" (Rom. 7:23). Saint James uses the same militant metaphor when he speaks of the "passions, which wage war in your members" (James 4:1). Concupiscence, which is the result of sin and which, as The Council of Trent tells us, remains after sin has been forgiven, is forever pulling down man's high aspirations exalted by God's grace.

That truth is the theological and psychological basis of the self-repression, self-discipline, self-conquest which penance means. Any Catholic will admit in theory that penance is necessary; but when he actually comes to reduce conviction to action, selfishness and whining human nature, couched in plush mediocrity, clamorously rebel. We keep our certitude about the need of penance comfortably vague. Many a Catholic, like the character in Duhamel, "would give his life, but not this slice of mutton." Or he may retrench like Newman's heroic trencherman who, on the vigil of Saint Peter, instructed his man: "Let us have a plain beefsteak and a saddle of mutton; no Portugal onions,

Watkins, or currant-jelly; and some simple pudding, Char-
lotte pudding, Watkins, that will do."

How different is the attitude of Saint Paul; unimpressed
by his own gigantic labors, he humbly admits: "I chastise
my body and bring it into subjection, lest perhaps after
preaching to others I myself should be rejected" (1 Cor.
9:27). We, too, must constantly remind ourselves of this
basic truth precisely because so many persuasive forces
deny it. The radio has convinced us that the luxurious is
ordinary and the superfluous necessary. Advertisements
extend to the human being that old slogan of the paint
company—"save the surface and you save all."

Paul points out, in the concluding lines of today's epistle,
our real greatness, our genuine glory: "You have received
a spirit of adoption as sons." We are sons of God, "heirs
also; heirs indeed of God and joint heirs with Christ." How
stupid it is then to concentrate on the body, which will some
day be the inheritance of worms; how stupid to cater
to its every whim, to sate its every desire, to repress it in
nothing—while we forget and neglect the soul.

Therefore Take Heed

I Corinthians 10:12

The books of the Bible, if we read them intelligently, are breathless adventure stories. In the section of First Corinthians which is the epistle for the Mass of the ninth Sunday after Pentecost, Saint Paul, in a series of quick references, recalls some exciting incidents.

We can see the encampment of the Israelites, their tents sprawled against the brooding backdrop of Sinai, wreathed in mists, haloed in thunders and lightnings. Beyond is the Red Sea, placid now, after its raised waters had billowed in to erase the miraculous highway and the pursuing Egyptians. The chosen people have been safely delivered from their enemies; God has guided them with a pillar of fire, a column of cloud; He has sent them quail, manna,

and water out of a rock. Yet four times it is explicitly recorded that they "murmured."

And now, as Moses communes with God on the mountain peak, they melt down their golden trinkets, fashion
a calf and adore it: "And the people sat down to eat and
drink, and they rose up to play" (Exodus 32:6). These
are the words which Paul quotes to his Corinthian Christians, some of whom still ate contaminated meat which had
been sacrificed to idols.

He gives other instances of man's infidelity and God's
anger. There was swift and severe punishment for carnal
sins with the daughters of Moab (Numbers 25). When
the stiff-necked people rebelled, "speaking against God and
Moses," a plague of serpents reduced them to prayerful
humility (Numbers 21). And from these and other examples Paul concludes: "Now all these things happened
to them as a type, and they were written for our correction,
upon whom the final age of the world has come."

The ancient Jews, therefore, were the beneficiaries of
God's munificence. The miracles whereby He protected,
fed, guided them into the Promised Land were types of the
sacraments to come in the New Law—the Messianic era
of salvation which Paul designates as "the final age of
the world." Notwithstanding God's loving care, the ungrateful people fell into sin and the all-merciful God, who
is also infinitely just, smote them with physical death.

We, likewise, who have the sacraments and other means
of grace which the New Dispensation affords, says Paul,
have the same faltering human will which tricked them
into sin. We must not presume; that is, fall into the spiritual stupidity of overconfidence. If we fail to profit by our
spiritual advantages, refusing to cooperate with the grace

and inspiration of the Holy Spirit, we shall die the eternal death that is perdition. "Therefore let him who thinks he stands take heed lest he fall," Paul ominously warns. But he immediately goes on to balance the admonition with assurance, establishing that perfect equilibrium which is our holy faith. "God is faithful and will not permit you to be tempted beyond your strength."

In these two mutually stabilizing concepts you have the real completeness of faith. There is no room for presumption: "Pride goeth before destruction, and the spirit is lifted up before a fall" (Prov. 16:18). But discouragement or despair has no place in the equation of faith either; for, as Paul says, quoting the Psalmist: "The Lord is my helper: I will not fear" (Heb. 13:6). Sustained by these complementary convictions, the apostle, who gloried only in his infirmities (2 Cor. 12:5), who exhorted his disciples to "work out your salvation in fear and trembling" (Phil. 2:12), and was himself most humble in his quest for God (1 Cor. 9:27), could nevertheless exult: "I can do all things in Him who strengthens me" (Phil. 4:14).

Our trouble is that we rely on our own resources. Then, when we find our strength insufficient for the struggle, we fall into discouragement which readily ripens into despair. The onslaught of temptation could find us armored and ready for battle if we turned to God. But alone, unarmed, we cannot sustain its impetus. We cannot go it alone nor can we hope for victory if we are not strong. With the swift strokes of a master's brush, Saint Luke (Luke 14:28-31) vividly catches the lesson of today's epistle: the lesson of the folly of presumption: "Which of you having a mind to build a tower, does not first sit down and reckon the charges that are necessary? Or what king, about to make war against another king, does not first sit down and think whether he be able?" So, too, we should not presume to be stronger than we are; we need help, assistance, aid. We cannot go it alone against the vile tide of human events; but with God's help, by divine assistance, we can with hearts of courage and hope of victory win each day's battle with God by our side.

The Spirit Is Given to Each One for Profit

I Corinthians 12:7

When the Church first began to convert the world to Christ, the laborers were few indeed, the vineyard vast and fallow. The Holy Spirit, therefore, illustrated and ratified the apostolic preaching with confirmatory miracles designed to shake the pagan world out of its spiritual grossness and to prepare men to listen respectfully and receptively to the good tidings of salvation. Thus Barnabas and Paul reporting to the "apostles and presbyters" in Jerusalem, on their missionary journeyings, told "of the great signs and wonders that God had done among the Gentiles through them" (Acts 15:12). Prominent among the signs and wonders which accompanied the early dissemination of the seed which is the word of God were those divine gifts and extraordinary endowments called *charismata*. Paul mentions them in the epistle for the Mass of the tenth Sunday after Pentecost, listing nine—among them the gifts of healing, working miracles and prophecy.

These spectacular gifts, rather common in the early days of struggle, have for the most part been withdrawn in our day. But, as Paul writes: "There are varieties of gifts, but the same Spirit; and there are varieties of ministries but the same Lord; and there are varieties of workings, but the same God who works all things in all." The changeless Trinity still operates in the individual soul. The timeless, supernatural dynamism of grace goes on undiminished. But though a Lourdes, Guadalupe or Fatima may jolt us out of our ordinary spiritual torpor for a while, the tragic fact is that normally we are insensitive to the marvelous supernatural activity within us.

Now, one adverts to the operations of grace in our souls only in prayer or periods of quiet thought; and for most of us, unhappily, such interludes are infrequent. Father Plus quotes the sage remark of René Schwob: "The present age has lost the secret of solitude." We romp riotously along on what Lewis Mumford called a plane of "hilarious anesthesia." We fear the dark halls of our own hollow interiors. We are a generation which "goes places and does things."

La Bruyère puts it bluntly: "Our whole trouble comes of never being able to be alone: hence, gaming, dissipation, wine, women, uncharity, envy, forgetfulness of oneself and of God." Even on the natural plane, a nation peopled by mindless mobs is in perilous plight, as Carlyle remarks in praise of "noble, silent men," of whom he says, "a country that has none or few of these is in a bad way." Supernaturally, such noisy superficiality is fatal indeed. "Millions may hurry along the streets of great cities absorbed in their business or pleasure or sorrows with never a thought of God," Pius XII once lamented, "yet the only true God is no less real; it is He who sustains them in their existence."

Yet even now we reserve to nuns and monks the idea of recollection, the deliberate advertence to the presence of God, the conscious cultivation of an interior climate of silence and serenity in which the inspirations of the Holy Spirit can be heard, a constant cloistering of the heart against the thronging clamors of the outside world. "Silence alone reveals the depths of life," wrote Maurice Zundel. It is, then, vitally important for each of us to withdraw occasionally from the world of rockets and roaring motors, screaming radios, black headlines and red sensations, to rest a while in the desert places of our own hearts.

"With desolation is all the land made desolate: because there is none that considereth in the heart," wrote the prophet centuries ago (Jer. 12:11). Contrast with that Our Lady, mother and model, who "kept in mind all these words, pondering them in her heart" (Luke 2:19).

Many of us alternate between the merely vacuous and the positively vapid. We seldom or never raise our minds and hearts to God or advert to the Trinity within our souls while in the state of grace. We walk as blind, unaware aliens through the supernatural wonders of the world within us, the world of God, of grace, of glory, begun here on earth and consummated in heaven—the miracle and mystery of our union with God in time that becomes the beatific vision of eternity.

Christ Died . . . Was Buried . . . Rose Again

I Corinthians 15:3-4

The ancient pagan, as Cardinal Wiseman has observed, had generally only the coldest idea of death. He would have appreciated the Anglo-Saxon metaphor for life: a bird winging out of the boisterous night passing briefly through the warm, bright banquet hall, then lost again in the enveloping blackness. The little life of man, Homer said, withers like a leaf. The Christian concept of resurrection, therefore, was to the sophisticated pagan as revolutionary as it was ridiculous; and the apostles made the Resurrection of Christ, which is a pledge of our own rising, the central point of their preaching (1 Cor. 15:14).

Paul, standing in the Areopagus of decadent Athens, ended his sermon to the supercilious philosophers there with a reference to the risen Christ and the final judgment of the world. "Now when they heard of a resurrection of the dead, some began to sneer, but others said: 'We will hear thee again on this matter'" (Acts 17:32). On trial before King Agrippa, Bernice and Festus, Paul returned to the same cardinal truth, and Festus "said with a loud voice, 'Paul, thou art mad; thy great learning is driving thee to madness'" (Acts 26:24).

In his first epistle to the Corinthians, part of which is read in the Mass for the eleventh Sunday after Pentecost, Paul is expounding this heart warming dogma, that Christ died and rose again: so we, Christ's brethren, shall, through His power and mercy, likewise triumph over the grave and over corruption.

One can readily imagine what explosive force this concept had upon minds steeped in the pessimistic pagan outlook. The new promise fulfilled man's highest hopes, erased his deepest glooms. Cicero had argued to some sort of immortality from the very ache and appetite for it which was one of man's deepest hungers. If there were no hope "of a continuation of life after death," he said, men would not die for their country, nobility would lose its basic motive.

How extremely penetrating that analysis was is evident from the lives of modern pagans who have jettisoned this belief. In Galsworthy's play, The Roof, Lennox cynically refers to death as "the eternal anesthetic"; in The Apple Tree, Ashurst says that after life "we go out like flames . . . we may flicker and cling about a bit, perhaps." It is difficult to see what good man can make of a life which is irretrievably extinguished by the grave-digger's shovel. Take this dogma of the resurrection away from man, wrote

Leo XIII, and he has no call "to endure toil and suffering."
He must find all his happiness here and so "every man will
naturally lay hands on all he can in the hope of living
happily on the spoils of others."

In today's section of his fifteenth chapter, Paul victori-
ously establishes the incontrovertible fact of Christ's resurrection; and the rest of the chapter exults in the fact that
we, too, shall rise gloriously. The body, like "a bare grain"
sown in dishonor, rises in glory; sown in weakness, it
rises in power. He contrasts the first man, Adam, who
brought sin into the world and was of the earth, earthy,
with the second Man, Christ, who brought salvation and
is from heaven, heavenly. "Therefore, even as we have
borne the likeness of the earthy, let us also bear the
likeness of the heavenly" (1 Cor. 15:1-49).

That was the constant ambition of the saints. The young
Italian nobleman Aloysius Gonzaga, to whom life beckoned
most enticingly, was forever asking himself: How does
this action square with my eternal destiny? The young
Polish aristocrat Stanislaus Kostka, continually reminded
himself: I was born for greater things. They made Paul's
words their own: "I strain forward to what is before, I
press on towards the goal, to the prize of God's heavenly
call in Christ Jesus" (Phil. 3:14), to heaven where Our
Lord awaits us and Our Lady, whose Assumption into
glory we commemorate at this time.

"For this world as we see it is passing away" (1 Cor.
7:31). The stable element in all the flux is man's soul,
which neither age can wither nor vicissitude dismay.
And both the Resurrection and the Assumption remind us
that even our poor bodies, badgered by germs, wearied by

suffering, will one day blossom into glory when faith is caught up in vision, hope bursts into fruition and only love remains.

He Made Us Fit Ministers

2 Corinthians 3:6

The impeccably suave and diplomatic Cardinal Consalvi, papal Secretary of State under Pius VII, was an abomination to Napoleon, whom he continually outwitted. In an angry outburst one day, the Corsican assured Consalvi that the Emperor's might was sufficient to destroy the Cardinal's Church. "Your Majesty," the Secretary replied with open humility and hidden humor, "not even we priests have achieved that in eighteen centuries!" It was a subtly theological reply, pointing out that divine guidance and support, not human prudence, learning or politics, had enabled the Church not only to survive but to flourish. It was also a revelation of the personal unworthiness which most priests feel when they contrast their own spiritual paltriness with the sublime vocation to which they have been called. Individually they have their faults. But the large and easy oversimplification of anticlericalism which depicts them all as bumptious and domineering is as gross an exaggeration as the fat monk with the foam-capped mug who is, for many people, an adequate symbol and summary of medieval monasticism.

Anticlericalism, either the open kind from enemies outside or the covert and genteel sort in which so many Catholics indulge today, is no new growth. Saint Paul had his detractors and calumniators, who mocked his message and sneered at his person and his preaching. In the Second Corinthians, part of which is read in the Mass for the twelfth Sunday after Pentecost, Paul vigorously vindicates his apostolate and indicates the source of his authority and assurance. It resides in no natural ability of his. Of himself, he is nothing. Supernaturally, he is deaf, mute and blind, unable even to conceive a salutary thought. "But our sufficiency is from God. He also it is who has made us fit ministers of the new covenant . . ."

We who are so prone to criticize priests might well meditate on those words. For the priest is to be respected not because he is personable, wise, cultured or learned. God grant he may have all those qualities; he should have them. But his real title to the deference of the faithful derives from his dogmatic position as "another Christ," a continuation of Our Lord in the world.

In his two specificative functions, the priest is depersonalized. He says "This is My Body: This is My Blood." And again, "I absolve you from your sins." In those utterances he speaks with the authority of Jesus Christ and in His name who made the priest a "fit minister of the new covenant." He is the timeless, nameless man in vestments: nameless, because when he dons the vestments, he doffs his own person and speaks as another Christ; timeless, because as he stands before the altar he is one with Augustine, Aquinas, Bonaventure, Ignatius, Francis Suarez—all of them, primarily and above everything, priests.

The priest lives a life of consecrated loneliness. He must walk in angelic purity through the foul floods of sin. He is a cynosure so that, as Saint John Chrysostom says, "It is impossible to conceal the faults of priests; even their smallest faults are manifest." Many of us are eager to leap on those manifest defects and exploit them as the subject matter of uncharitable talk. The reaction of Saint Teresa of Avila, that supremely great realist, is so much more wholesome. She asks her nuns to pray for priests "that Our Lord may protect them in their great warfare, so that they may escape the many dangers of the world."

The priest should be a man of God (1 Tim. 6:11), detached like Melchisedech from all earthly ties (Heb. 7:2), God's helper (1 Cor. 3:9) and ambassador (2 Cor. 5:20), a defender of the faith (Phil. 1:16). He must be a man of great sanctity, as Popes Pius X and Pius XI have insisted. The priesthood is a difficult vocation. The wonder of it is not that some have fallen short, but that, human nature being what it is, many more, with God's help, have not. If you must talk about priests, therefore, talk about them prayerfully to God, not spitefully to men; ask God's Providence over them that they may always walk worthy of their vocation.

Is the Law Contrary to the Promises of God?

Galatians 3:21

Professor Irwin Edman, in his book *Fountainheads of Freedom*—written in collaboration with Herbert Schneider —gives short shrift to what he calls "Intimations of Democracy in the Christian Tradition." In the three hundred pages of confirmatory texts which he cites, he allots three pages and a half to the Gospels, three to Saint Paul and a half page to Saint James. He does not mention Saint Augustine except cursorily and almost contemptuously. Saint Thomas Aquinas comes in briefly. John of Salisbury and Marsilio of Padua represent the Middle Ages; Bellarmine and Suarez do not rate mention.

Now all this is not to review an aging book or to rebuke a bookman, but to concretize a prevalent attitude: namely, that one would vainly look to Catholic thinkers for any valid ideas on liberty or freedom.

Yet the epistle for the thirteenth Sunday after Pentecost is another of Paul's passionate pleas for freedom. Professor Edman notes the irony that "Paul of Tarsus, in many ways an uncompromising fanatic . . . the most narrow of men, should have been the influential exponent of the idea of the brotherhood of man." Paul, the professor reveals, "was a Greek in education" and into the idea of brotherhood he incorporated "a mystical note that he owed not so much to his Jewish heritage as to his Greek environment." In that snarl of loose writing and simple inaccuracy, the one shining word is "uncompromising." That Paul certainly was.

The occasion of his letter was the schism among his beloved Galatians caused by those vexatious doctrinaires the Judaizers, who contended that even converts were still under the burden of the Old Law. Paul had always preached the liberty of the sons of God. Now he writes an epistle which is one of the finest outpourings of the human spirit. It is stern, tender, passionate, plaintive: an example, as Father Prat says, of Paul's "incorrect, breathless phrases, bending under their weight of ideas." The Law, Paul says, was supplanted by the living Lord. The Law was a temporary stopgap in man's religious experience. Christ is the truth (John 14:6) and He has said, "The truth shall make you free" (John 8:32).

Paul was an exponent of liberty, not of libertarianism. He did not look on religion as a choice of temperament. He knew that Christ would not leave us hundreds of sects so that the individual might shop around and find one suitable to his personality. Gethsemane and Calvary show us a Man desperately in earnest about His message, and to Paul the road to God was as unwavering as the *Via Dolorosa*. It was impossible, in the nature of things, that one road should be as good as another. To him (to change the metaphor), the tree of theology grew as straight as the cross. It did not ramify into many branches from any of which, as from the limbs of Zachaeus' sycamore, man might apprehend and achieve Christ. Christ's Church is, and must be, just as uncompromising as its Founder.

"Indeed it is one of the most popular charges . . . that she is 'incorrigible,'" Newman wrote; "change she cannot, if we listen to Saint Athanasius or Saint Leo; change she never will, if we believe the controversialist or alarmist of the present day." Paul had anathematized even an angel who would preach a gospel different from his (Gal. 1:8). So, too, with great tolerance and hate for bigotry, we cooperate with our fellow-citizens in social, economic and political affairs—the great areas of civic liberty. But as faithful followers of Christ, we must never dim or dilute the dogmas for which Christ lived and died.

They Who Belong to Christ

Galatians 5:24

Euphuism and Euphemism are two modes of thought and expression having both similarities and dissimilarities. "Euphuism" derives from John Lyly's sixteenth-century novel *Euphues*—a work of embroidered elegance and scented stylistic obesity—and it signifies bloated affectation in writing. "Euphemism" is a minor item in our heritage from Greece, and designates a manner of thinking and speaking which melts hard facts and wraps ugly realities in the velvet of roundabout verbiage.

Whatever the literary critic may say about them, euphuism and euphemism are definitely dangerous when they invade the terminology of theology, either dogmatic or moral. For they dull the sharp edges of truths which themselves should be emblematically apprehended; they substitute misleading synonyms for other matters which are nasty and should be known as such. Thus, when a philosopher writes: "We are driven by ineluctable necessity to postulate the existence of a supreme energy," John Lyly's spirit quivers with a ghostly jealousy. Asked if he thought there was a "personal God," one prominent Protestant theologian replied: "All we can say in that regard is that there is a personality-producing force or forces in the universe." Others speak of "pre-marital chastity" as a tabu, glorify an actress' fourth marriage as a triumph of clean young love, dismiss all self-discipline as unwholesome inhibition, and make natural impulse the only imperative in human life. Such euphuists and euphemists are doing real harm. They confuse clear issues and canonize the contemptible with a halo of hazy words.

They might well take Saint Paul as a stylistic model. In the epistle for the fourteenth Sunday after Pentecost, he contrasts the fruits of the Spirit and the fruits of the flesh in blunt, biting language. The Spirit and the flesh are, he says, at war. The works of the flesh are manifest—"immorality, uncleanness, licentiousness, idolatry, witchcrafts, enmities . . . anger . . . envies, murders, drunkenness, carousings, and such like." And he repeats his previous, plain warning that "they who do such things will not attain the kingdom of God." On the other hand, "the fruit of the Spirit is: charity, joy, peace, patience, kindness, goodness, long-suffering, mildness, faith, modesty, continency, chastity."

Today, even the most militant optimist is forced to admit that much is wrong with the world. If he were to list those disruptive forces which keep our times in a ferment, his list would practically coincide with Paul's itemization of the works of the flesh: immorality, jealousies, quarrels, factions, parties, envies. It would seem that in our world the flesh is ascendant, the Spirit in eclipse.

Imagine the earth as it would be if the Spirit were triumphant—a world of charity, joy, peace, patience, kindness, long-suffering, mildness. But we shall not attain such a goal merely through conferences, classes in personal magnetism or resolutions in the Rotary clubs. The Church reminds us of that in the prayer for this Sunday's Mass: "Keep, we beseech Thee, O Lord, Thy Church in Thy perpetual mercy: and because without Thee the weakness of man is wont to fall, save him by Thine aid from all things harmful, and guide him to all things profitable for salvation."

Man of his own weight and concupiscent drag may fall into sin and the slavery of the flesh. But man sustained and supported by God can harvest the fruits of the Spirit. What of you personally? What is the dominant impetus in your soul, your life—the Spirit or the flesh? "They who belong to Christ have crucified their flesh with its passions and desires" (Gal. 5:24). There can be no compromise, for as Christ warns us in the gospel: "He who is not with me is against me, and he who does not gather with me scatters" (Matt. 12:30).

What a Man Sows That Will He Also Reap

Galatians 6:8

A colloquialism common to both adults and adolescents is the contemptuous dismissal of an arrogant person with the phrase: "He thinks he's something!" By intonation and intent, the remark conveys the idea that the minor Malvolio at whom it is directed is the only one who holds that erroneous opinion. Probably few who employ the expression realize that they are substantially quoting the words of Saint Paul in that section of Galatians read in the Mass for the fifteenth Sunday after Pentecost. "For if anyone thinks himself to be something, whereas he is nothing, he deceives himself." Paul never tired of reiterating that basic truth of supernatural life that without God man is spiritually inept, an orphan, an alien, a pauper, even more, a corpse. Christ unmistakably established this truth at the Last Supper: "Without Me, you can do nothing" (John 15:5).

Paul's whole passage is a blunt rebuke to the vaunting and vaulting egoism so common today. It is a plea for humility, meekness, charity and the recognition of one's own weakness. A modern type frequently encountered is the man who makes a creed of Emersonian "self-reliance" and, like Henley, imagines himself the master of his fate, the captain of his soul. He measures success by the number of lines he has in *Who's Who* and would rather have his name in the *Blue Book* than in the book of life. He is haughty in speech. When he opens his oracular mouth, let no dog bark. He may laugh at the idea of papal infallibility—which, of course, he has never taken the trouble to understand—while he invests his own utterances with a defiant and decretal finality. He is in love with himself and must show off his beloved to a waiting world, even hiring press agents to help him do so.

In his *Three Reformers,* Jacques Maritain puts a merciless finger on the core of two minds which have profoundly influenced history in the last four hundred years. Of Martin Luther he says that his chief characteristic was radical egoism: "Luther's self becomes practically the center of gravity of everything, especially in the spiritual order." Likewise he sums up Rousseau: "Self, self, divine self, always self, it is always in himself that Jean-Jacques would have beatitude." Carlyle had previously reached that same conclusion: "The fault and misery of Rousseau was what we easily name by a single word, *egoism.*" Luther and Rousseau did much to shape modern patterns of thought, of which one is surely egoism.

Even though we are continually warned by the gospels about self-love, and even though we know from the *Imitation of Christ* "that the love of thyself hurts thee more than anything in the world," we can still ignore the warning. If we are in the state of grace, we have Christ actually within us. We are Christocentric. But, through spiritual fatuousness, we can remain psychologically egocentric. This is our great weakness and the fault lies in ourselves that we are weaklings.

Which of us does not know the Catholic—and for many of us the knowledge comes from self-knowledge—who is demanding, impatient or lordly with a clerk, waiter or gasoline-station attendant? Extremely sensitive himself, such a person forgets the feelings of his fellows, is openly disdainful of his "inferiors," secretly scornful of those toward whom expediency requires him to maintain the outer guise of courtesy. He despises those of a race, color or social class other than his own. He is press agent for himself, regarding praise of another as a personal slur, never missing the chance to depreciate any achievement not his own. Upon his sterile soul the exhortation of Saint Paul falls vainly: "Bear one another's burdens, and so you will fulfill the law of Christ."

"Be not deceived, God is not mocked," Paul sternly warns us; "for what a man sows, that he will also reap." Self-love is the greatest of deceits; the lover and beloved are alike fraudulent. It is unproductive. It leaves no room for God. And the soul which has loved only itself in life may well have only itself for all eternity.

My Tribulations Are Your Glory

Ephesians 3:13

To Cicero, the crucifixion of a Roman citizen was such an unspeakable atrocity that he frankly confessed himself unable to characterize it adequately. Certainly the great rhetorician's power of expression would have sputtered into wordlessness had he faced the problem of describing the crucifixion of God for the salvation of men, the death of Jesus which is our life. Because of that vivifying death, the cross, so abhorrent to Cicero and the civilized ancients, has become the symbol dearest to the Christian heart. It is the "symbol of the Lord," as Clement of Alexandria wrote with pregnant simplicity; it is the *Vexilla Regis*, "the standard of the King," as the Church triumphantly sings: it was the flaming emblem under which Constantine crushed Maxentius and opened a new phase of history; it will be the blazing oriflamme of Christ's second, judicial coming in the twilight of the world.

Little wonder, then, that the Church's liturgy is illuminated with frequent feasts in honor of the cross. Her Good Friday rite revolves around it; in May she commemorates the finding of the true cross; through the golden haze of September she directs the prayerful attention of the faithful once again towards Calvary, by the feast of the Exaltation of the Holy Cross.

That feast is one of the most ancient in the Church's calendar, and great devotion to the cross was always characteristic of the Catholic. It was central in Paul's thinking: "but we, for our part, preach a crucified Christ" (1 Cor. 1:23) and "I determined not to know anything among you, except Jesus Christ and him crucified" (1 Cor. 2:5). The Introit of the feast is taken from Paul: "But as for me, God forbid that I should glory save in the cross of our Lord Jesus Christ" (Gal. 6:14); while the Epistle is his exhortation to the Philippians not merely to admire Christ's generosity but to emulate it: "Let this mind be in you, which was also in Christ Jesus" who "humbled himself, becoming obedient unto death, even to the death of the cross" (Phil. 2:5-9).

When the early pagans, sharing Cicero's loathing of the cross, contemptuously called the Christians "cross-worshippers," their insult was received as an accolade. Tertullian, in fact, identified the Christians as "devotees of the cross"; and the same writer declared: "We Christians wear out our foreheads with the sign of the cross." Every time we make the sign of the cross, which many of us do so carelessly and thoughtlessly, we proclaim ourselves devotees of the cross, accepting all the difficult implications of that "doctrine of the cross" which "is foolishness to those who perish, but to those who are saved, that is, to us, it is the power of God" (1 Cor. 1:18).

No one can look at the cross without beholding her who stood so close to it, who shared so stingingly in her Son's agony. Some of the loveliest feasts of Our Lady are liturgical settings for this commemoration of the cross. September eighth we observed her birthday; on the twelfth we rejoiced in her sweet name; and on the day following the Exaltation of the Cross we recall her seven sorrows. The prayer of Saint Paul in the very consoling words of today's epistle were but the echo of Mary's prayer for us on Calvary: "I pray you not to be disheartened by my tribulations for you, for they are your glory."

Look back in meditation again at Calvary, emerging like an obscene, gigantic skull from the chilly, mid-afternoon dusk. The forked lightnings reveal a dying man. Beside Him, pale, heart-broken, adoring, stands His mother. Can you turn away unimpressed, uninspired; can you resume a life which denies all that He taught like those whom Saint Paul mentions: "they" who "crucify again for themselves the Son of God and make him a mockery?" (Heb. 6:6). Crucifixion is a shameful death, but it is a mockery, tragic and terrible, when Christ has died in vain for those whom He loved—you and me and all generations of mankind. Trials and tribulations are the lot of all of us but they are glorified in the sufferings of Christ Crucified when we stand bravely with His Mother and see in His death new life, fresh strength and renewed hope.

Walk in a Manner Worthy of Your Calling

Ephesians 4:1

The Seventeenth Sunday after Pentecost yields precedence on occasion to the feast of Saint Matthew, apostle and evangelist. Coincidentally, the epistle for the Sunday contains a text on which Matthew's life was a concrete commentary. Paul, writing from prison, exhorts the Ephesians "to walk in a manner worthy of the calling with which you were called, with all humility and meekness, with patience, bearing with one another in love, careful to preserve the unity of the Spirit in the bond of peace" (Eph. 4:1-4). Matthew certainly walked in a manner worthy of his calling.

The gospels in the Mass for the vigil and the feast of Saint Matthew both recall his vocation. Levi, son of

Alpheus he was (Mark 2:14), a Jewish tax-gatherer in the employ of Herod Antipas, one of those publicans whom all Pharisees despised (Matt. 9:11). One day as he sat in the toll booth (Luke 5:27), a shadow fell on Levi and a voice struck into his heart like a silver sword: "Follow me." Levi the publican disappeared into thin air; it was Matthew the apostle who arose and walked after the Master, never again to turn back. He left all things, because he had discovered the one thing necessary (Luke 10:42).

We who attach so much importance to money might well meditate on the fact that Matthew would seem to have been the logical candidate for treasurer of the apostolic band, because of his previous financial experience. But it would appear that he cut himself off completely from the bright and blinking witchery of gold; that he was perfectly content to have Judas carry the purse. Thereafter he concentrated on walking "in a manner worthy of the calling with which [he was] called." History is reticent about him; after the dispersion of the apostles, legend tells us that he preached the faith in Ethiopia—not the Nubian country we know, but an area south of the Caspian Sea; and like his brethren, he sealed his message with his martyrdom.

Obviously there are two kinds of vocation indicated here; Paul is talking to laymen and telling them to walk in a manner worthy of their calling; whereas Matthew was summoned to the priestly and episcopal apostolate. That is an important point for, as Father O'Connor has pointed out in his admirable book *The Layman's Call,* "vocation . . . belongs to the laity as well as to the clergy or the religious." All are called by God, as Jacques Maritain writes, "to the precept of tending—each one according to his own status—toward the perfection of charity, as toward the aim of life."

There is, of course, the *special* and higher vocation to complete self-dedication in religion; there is the *special* vocation to the priesthood. We must avoid the muddy and undogmatic thinking which reduces all states to a dead level of drab neutrality, erasing priesthood and hierarchy, all distinctions and dignities. But, that being said, it is still true that you personally have a vocation, whether you are married or single, a doctor, lawyer or Indian chief. Christ has called you to be a *Catholic* doctor, a *Catholic* lawyer, a *Catholic* Indian chief, to work out your faith in whatever department of endeavor is yours, to be a leaven in the mass.

This means that you must have that interior love of Christ which overflows in apostolic action and example, as Pius XI intimated in one of his many descriptions of Catholic Action. Its agents, he says, are "*called* by a singular grace of God," to a "function which is not far removed from the sacerdotal office." You hear a man say "I didn't have a vocation," and he means a vocation to the priesthood. Actually, however, he has a vocation to be a militant, intelligent Catholic.

Many of us might well re-evaluate our Catholicism in terms of vocation. For the Sunday Catholic completely misses the point if he leaves his faith in mothballs when he goes out to buy and sell, to practise law or medicine, to act as employer, employe, labor leader, politician or elevator operator. He does not walk in a manner worthy of the calling in which he was called, if he fails to put first things first. He has been first called to practise Catholicism.

We must then beware of the leaven of hypocrisy for

there is nothing "spoken in darkness" that shall not be "published in the light," nor "spoken in the ear" that "shall not be preached from the housetops" (Luke 12:1-3). Every shady deal and every whispered plot is a sin against the vocation to which we are called, "for a man's life does not consist in an abundance of things" as his first and foremost possession. We must, then, first seek the kingdom of God and His justice and after that on the promise of God "all things else shall be added" unto us.

Made Rich in Him

I Corinthians 1:5

Monsignor Knox suggests the stimulating possibility that
if we were allowed to meet any Old Testament personage
of our own choosing, he would select King David. For,
he explains, "with all the lawless faults of his age and
character, there are still a freshness and a graciousness
about . . . him which make him seem real to us, and . . .
lovable." Be that as it may, there is no genuine graciousness, natural or supernatural, which does not include a
capacity for gratitude; and that David unquestionably had.
It was he who appointed the Levites "to stand in the morning to give thanks, and to sing praises to the Lord" (1 Par.
23:30); the theme of thanksgiving pulses through the
Psalms (Ps. 108:30); and one of his most masterful lyric

outpourings welled from this same source (2 Kings, 22).

Saint Paul, who often cited David and included him among the great men to whom he paid immortal tribute in one of his finest passages (Heb. 11:32-39), likewise had David's constant sense of divine beneficence and the correlative of profound gratitude. This spirit breathes through the opening lines of his First Epistle to the Corinthians, read in the Mass for the eighteenth Sunday after Pentecost. "I give thanks to my God always for you, for the grace of God that is given you in Christ Jesus, that in all things you are made rich in him. . . ." We who take God and His goodness so much for granted, who fall into the subtle heresy of attributing all success to self and all failure to some insuperable and undeserved fate, might meditate profitably on those words. "For nothing is so acceptable to God," Saint John Chrysostom assures us, "as that men should be thankful, both for themselves and for others." And for this reason, Chrysostom concludes, Saint Paul prefaces every epistle with a reminder of the need and duty of gratitude.

Saint Bernard was eloquently insistent on this primary but neglected obligation. Just as the sea is the ultimate source of all springs and rivers, so the Lord Jesus Christ is the fountainhead of all benefits; "the continence of the flesh, the energy of the heart, the rectitude of the will, all flow from that spring." But we who are the recipients of infinite mercy and goodness, who, when we pray at all, ask only for future favors with no advertence to past gifts, place ourselves with the nine ungrateful lepers who were so intoxicated with the gift of health that they forgot to return and thank the Giver of health (Luke 17:17).

Thereby we diminish or even dam the stream of divine

generosity flowing into our souls. "He who is faithful in
returning due thanks to God shall be accounted worthy
of greater benefits," says Saint Bernard. You do yourself
a favor by thanking God for His goodness; He desires to
be thanked—"not," as Bernard insists, "because there is
anything wanting to Christ," but because by our gratitude
we follow the higher dictates of nature and grace and so
make ourselves eligible for further endowments.

If a man does you a kindness, if he makes you a present,
if he gives you a dinner, decency and courtesy require you
to acknowledge your indebtedness. The ugly epithet "ingrate" is not one which a civilized man would lightly endure. Yet Christ by His life, passion and death redeemed
you; by baptism He has raised you to supernatural life;
when your infidelity dragged you into sin, His sacrament
of penance revived and restored you; He blessed your wedding and is the Unseen Friend of your married life; He
waits in His tabernacle to receive you in prayerful audience
or, better still, for you to receive Him in Holy Communion;
He will stand beside your bed in that dread hour when
death will dim your eyes so that they may open on the
dazzling prospect of life and light eternal.

What of your gratitude? Do you ever thank Him, pay
Him a visit, attend the Holy Sacrifice voluntarily, receive
Him in Holy Communion? Or do you, who would resent
being regarded as an "ingrate" by men, care little how you
appear before Christ the Lord?

Do not Let the Sun Go Down

Ephesians 4:26

If a surrealist were to depict anger, he might well represent it as a twisted and throbbing heart out of which grow two hands; one clenched into a fist, the other clutching a dagger. For anger, in its extreme, is a faceless, mindless force, its language vituperation, its purpose vengeance. There is, of course, a justified anger; and such was the majestic rage of Moses when, descending from the mountain where he had communed with God, the tables of the Law in his hands, he found the frivolous people worshiping a golden calf. "And being very angry, he threw the tables out of his hands and broke them" (Exodus 32:19). Elbowing his way through the singing, dancing throng, he unceremoniously dethroned and destroyed the idol.

Similarly Our Lord, expelling the buyers and sellers from His Father's house, was motivated by a just and righteous indignation at their profanation of that sacred spot (Mark 11:15).

We, who are often shaken by resentment, like to imagine that our wrath, too, is disinterested and defensive of outraged justice, though a little self-scrutiny would soon convince us that it generally stems from pique, because someone has invaded one of our pet prejudices. Saint Paul, in the section of Ephesians read in the Mass for the nineteenth Sunday after Pentecost, warns his disciples against the malevolent mentality, the un-Christian explosion of the soul, which is anger. "Be angry and do not sin; do not let the sun go down upon your anger."

Realistically enough, this profound psychologist admits that the human soul is quick to resent, irritable, prone to take umbrage. But the spiritual difficulty comes when anger smolders into a desire for revenge. Dismiss your dudgeon at once, Paul advises; do not take it to bed with you; do not brood over it, storing it in the vaults of your memory until an opportunity arises to even the score.

Life would certainly be much more lightsome if people heeded that sage advice. Everyone knows of families split into factions, fighting an intramural civil war with husband against wife, or child opposing parent. All too familiar is the silly feud which makes Catholics pass each other without speaking or permits them to break their uncharitable silence only with intervals of articulate acrimony.

Towards the end of his life, Ignatius of Loyola, who in his youth had a fierce, flaming temper, was so meek that observers could not imagine him as he had been before grace and self-conquest had chastened him. Francis de Sales, likewise, through prayer, God's help and constant self-repression, raised the boiling-point of his blood above the heat of the day; and it was he who wrote the sagacious words: "We must have patience with the whole world, and most of all with ourselves. As soon as you begin to exercise yourself a little in patience, everything will move along splendidly; for the meek and loving Redeemer, who has inspired us with an ardent desire to serve Him, will furnish us with opportunities to do so."

There is the real motive for patience and every other virtue—the imitation of Christ. It was Paul's argument also, for in this negative section of Ephesians he is advocating no mere humanitarian self-control, the how-to-get-along-with-people idea. He is insisting rather on the dogmatic results of our incorporation in Christ, of our being "members of one another."

Recall Christ's patience in the face of insult (Mark 3:22); see Him submit voluntarily to the rabble in Gethsemane (Luke 22:54), watch Him stand silent before the Sanhedrin while the perjured witnesses babble their contradictions. Majestically sad and wordless He was when Herod's hall rang with mocking laughter and, through the red hours of His Passion, Isaias' words were amply verified: "He shall be led as a sheep to the slaughter and shall be dumb as a lamb before his shearer" (Isaias 53:7). But we are sensitive, prone to temper, quick to rage. Rarely, or at any rate, too rarely do we imitate Christ, who was the model for those saints whom we admire.

Making the Most of Your Time

Ephesians 5:16

An imbecile might be loosely described as a man alien to the normal, who makes a career of what ordinary people regard as foolishness. The madness of carnival is to him a native climate; the distorting mirrors of the amusement park are windows opening on the only reality he recognizes; a roller-coaster roaring at breakneck speed to no destination seems to him the most marvelous mode of travel to the best conceivable goal. We pity the feeble-minded person and we carefully avoid any personal actions which might lead people to look on us as "odd" or "peculiar." But even with all our care for personal dignity and decorum there can coexist a spiritual fatuity which threatens us, not with the loss of social standing and the laughter of men, but with the forfeiture of salvation and the eternal mockery of the demons.

So it is that Saint Paul, in the epistle for the twentieth Sunday after Pentecost, warns us in words of unblinking bluntness against this supernatural stupidity. The days are evil, he says; he advises all to "walk with care: not as unwise but as wise, making the most of your time . . . therefore do not become foolish, but understand what the will of the Lord is." He had previously summed up the obligations of the Christian as a child of light, a member of Christ, a recipient of the divine doctrine. The dogmatic grandeur of the individual, he now adds, imposes great responsibilities. Spiritual aimlessness is most reprehensible in one who has within him, by the divine indwelling, Jesus the Way. Spiritual insanity is unthinkable for the man who is a member of Jesus the Truth. Spiritual debility is inexcusable in an adopted brother of Jesus the Life.

Yet we need look no farther than our own hearts to see that such spiritual treachery to God and to ourselves is possible, even easy. We want to avoid the idiocy of the imbecile, to be sure; we desire to make successes of our lives. But we forget that the only way to make a success of human life is to fulfill in it what the Author of Life demands. We forget or forego the sage advice of Saint Paul: "Understand what the will of the Lord is." In designing life, God did not make an arbitrary or whimsical gesture; He gave life its shape and purposes; and it is only by conforming ourselves to that outline and by achieving those divinely appointed ends that we can make our lives successful.

Against all this is the clamorous objection of the world, with its own ideas of successful living. Dives is the hero of the worldling—Dives who had a full stomach, a full bankbook, who dined sumptuously and dressed luxuriously. Those whose eyes are bent on this earth, who can never see ultimates because of their exclusive preoccupation with the here and the now, can conveniently forget the timeless and terrific drawback in Dives' success story—that he died and went to Hell. Lazarus, outside this rich man's manor, clad in rags, his only roof the sky, his only walls the far horizons, too weak to dispute with the snapping village curs for the crumbs from the sybaritic board, is no hero to the man inoculated with the worldly idea of success. Disgust at the contemplation of Lazarus' rags and sores during life blinds the worldling to the eternal fact that rags and sores have been transmuted into the accoutrements of his glory forever.

"For the doctrine of the cross is foolishness to those who perish," wrote Saint Paul to the Corinthians and, in a later passage, "the foolishness of God is wiser than men, and the weakness of God is stronger than men" (I Cor. 1:18-25). This is a hard saying; without intense faith, we shall not subscribe to the paradoxically powerful "weakness of God," with its implications of humility, self-effacement, apparent foolishness and true success.

The Armor of God

Ephesians 6:11

The basic, irretrievable error that a strategist can make is to underestimate the strength of his enemy and so send his forces into battle casually overconfident. The swelling letter of Darius to Alexander, accompanied by the sarcastic gift of "a scourge and a ball . . . the latter, that you may amuse yourself . . . the former, to serve for your chastisement," was an invitation to doom for the man who boasted his "dominion of the earth." Alexander broke Darius at Faristan and Arbela.

Our Lord Himself pointed out the folly of self-assurance when He praised the wisdom of the king who, before joining battle, analyzed his resources and, finding himself overwhelmed, sent an embassy to negotiate a compromise

peace (Luke 14:31). And since that stout warrior of God
Job, who scored a notable victory over the enemy, has reminded us that the life of man on earth is a warfare (Job
7:1), we find Saint Paul in the epistle for the twenty-first
Sunday after Pentecost warning us of the foe arrayed
against us, the "monstrous regiment" in Mr. Hollis' phrase,
which we must face. "For our wrestling is not against flesh
and blood, but against the Principalities and the Powers . . .
against the wiles of the devil."

Back in the golden, purple garden of Paradise, which
Augustine so nostalgically describes in the *City of God,*
the devil successfully began his campaign against our race.
He seduced Eve, our common mother and made her the
agent in Adam's downfall. Skillfully inflaming her imagi-
nation, Satan induced her to translate God's forthright
declarative into a comfortable subjunctive. God had said:
"In what day soever thou shalt eat . . . thou shalt die the
death" (Gen. 2:17). That unequivocal threat Eve softened
into a sentimental possibility, giving as the reason for God's
prohibition, "Lest perhaps we die" (Gen. 3:3). As soon
as the devil saw her lapse into that most basic of all heresies,
the willingness to *reword* and *revise* God's mandate, he
was sure of victory. She fell, dragged Adam down with
her and the damage was done.

Unfortunately we reveal our ancestry and our derivation
from Eve by imitating her arrogance. Dalliance with the
devil means disaster, and Christ's curt "Begone, Satan"
(Matt. 4:10) rises too slowly to our lips. The "old serpent,"
as Saint John calls him (Apoc. 12:9), whose bloated boast
it was that he would "be like the most High" (Isaias
14:14), encourages us to underestimate him; the man off
guard is easy to conquer. The devil heartily indorses the

idea that he is part myth, part medieval mist, part bogey-
man, because then men will not take him seriously. "The
devil," writes Father Plus, "is not amusing. He can amuse;
which is something quite different. Not that he has in
himself a power of attraction, but because there is in us
a power of misunderstanding and illusion."

Newman was convinced that the devil had deceived
the modern world by promising it "knowledge, science,
philosophy, enlargement of mind." The devil "shows you
how to become as gods. Then he laughs and jokes with
you . . . gets intimate with you . . . takes your hand, and
gets his fingers between yours, and grasps them, and then
you are his." M. Maritain sees evidence of real diabolism
in present society, a subtle and sophisticated discipleship to
the demon. Centuries ago, Saint Paul called Satan "the
god of this world" (2 Cor. 4:4). He is no quaint legend
but a personal foe, with a twisted, angelically ingenious
intellect, tenacious, crafty, easily able to outwit you if
you face him without divine help, if you underestimate
him.

"Therefore," says Saint Paul, "take unto you the armor
of God . . . the breastplate of justice . . . the shield of
faith . . . the helmet of salvation and the sword of the
spirit (which is the word of God)." Thus accoutred you
are invulnerable, inviolable.

We Have Our Redemption through His Blood

Colossians 1:14

Indissolubly associated with the idea of kingliness is the notion of aloofness. The king is a man unique, hedged about with protocol, above and apart from the throng, enthroned in solitary splendor, outlined in regal ermine. All the more striking therefore is the accessibility of the King of Kings, Jesus Christ, whose absolute sovereignty we salute this Sunday. This is vividly evident in the first description of His Kingdom, sketched on the Mount of Beatitudes; and Saint Paul contrasts that scene with Sinai.

In the revelation of the Old Law God was hidden in rolling thunders; Moses, "terrified and trembling," was the mediator; the commandments were inscribed on tablets of stone and were so phrased as to emphasize rather the penalty of disobedience than the reward of compliance. On the Mount of Beatitudes Christ Himself, God and Man, was mediator; He sat in simple proximity to the pressing throngs, and announced that His law which would be engraved "in the fleshly tablets of the heart" (2 Cor. 3:3). Sinai is loud with the minatory phrase "Thou shalt not"; but the first word from the lips of the new Lawgiver is "Blessed" (Heb. 12:18-24).

All through His life, Christ was readily approachable, from the night when shepherds knelt in adoration until the black afternoon when the repentant thief implored mercy. All through the ages He has remained within easy reach; in His sacraments, His tabernacles, in the souls of the just. He is not far from anyone of us (Acts 17:27).

Correlative to the idea of king is that of queen. We cannot long meditate on the King of Heaven and earth without recalling her whom He so exalted to be His consort, especially in this, her month of October. And here again we find the accessibility of the King re-emphasized, for Mary is not only Queen and Mother, but mediatrix as well.

In the Old Testament, we read that Adonais, desiring to obtain a favor from King Solomon and being humbly hesitant to face the regal presence, went to Bethsabee, the king's mother, and enlisted her aid. She agreed to present the petition to her royal son, who received her with every mark of affectionate reverence and enthroned her "on his right hand." When he heard the nature of her errand, "the king said to her: My mother, ask: for I must not turn away thy face" (3 Kings 2:13-20). In the office of Mary's mediation, the Church puts into her Son's mouth those beautiful and filial words of Solomon. Cana shows us her influence, which is so great that it has been called "suppliant omnipotence."

"Let us venerate her from the depths of our hearts," cries Bernard, her great apostle, "and in all our prayers, for this is the desire of Him who wills that we receive everything through Mary." "From the moment she conceived the Word of God . . ." says Bernardine of Siena, "she obtained a certain jurisdiction, a sort of authority over every temporal possession of the Holy Spirit, to such an extent that we receive the grace of God only through Mary." Pius X declared: "Mary is the heavenly channel through which all graces descend to earth." Fifty-odd years ago, Leo XIII wrote: "By reason of her consent to divine motherhood, we may with equal justice assert that . . . nothing is bestowed upon us except through Mary," an opinion which Benedict XV ratified. Only a few years ago Pius XI was begging us to revive devotion to Mary's rosary, as the remedy for the ills then threatening the world.

Turn your eyes and your soul to Christ the King and Mary, His Queen. Hanging on the cross, beneath the inscription "Jesus of Nazareth, King of the Jews," He won redemption and salvation for us. But she who was standing beneath His cross during those horrible hours is the stewardess and dispenser of His infinite riches. They are ours for the asking, the seeking (Luke 11:9), as we renew our fealty to the King, our filial love for the Queen on this feast of Christ the King.

Our Citizenship Is in Heaven

Philippians 3:20

Polybius, in one swift, compact sentence, compressed the history of a nation's decadence and death. "In Carthage," he wrote, "no one is blamed, however he may have gained his wealth." Quoting that, Agnes Repplier comments incisively: "A pleasant place, no doubt, for business enterprise; a place where young men were taught to get on, and extravagance kept pace with shrewd finance. A self-satisfied place, self-confident, money-getting, woman-loving people, honoring success and hugging their fancied security, while in far-off Rome Cato pronounced their doom."

Her words recall A. Conan Doyle's story, *The Last Galley,* which pictures the Carthaginians assembled on a height watching a lone ship of their fleet approach. Was she a courier of victory over Rome? The question was answered by a fast, lithe Roman raider which slid out of the horizon to overtake, shatter and sink this lone survivor of Carthage's great navy.

As he traveled around the world, Mr. Belloc tells us, he was fascinated by the wayside remnants and relics of history, but "one has impressed me most. It was the simple plank which bore painted upon it, rather roughly, the single word 'Carthage.'" On what is now a sand-swept, sun-scourged hill, Scipio had declaimed Homer while the flames licked and crackled around "the towers of that imperial city that radiated over the Mediterranean and drew to itself the luxury and the wealth of every shore."

It is an arresting array of considerations, a possible parallel which educators might well present to American students, a meditation which all of us might profitably make.

Writing to his Philippian converts, in a section read as epistle in the Mass for the twenty-third Sunday after Pentecost, Paul characterizes those people who have the Carthaginian outlook: "Their end is ruin, their god is their belly, their glory is their shame, they mind the things of earth." And a civilization which rises and falls to the barometric readings of the cash-register and ticker-tape cannot shrug off those words.

"Our citizenship is in heaven," Paul adds by way of contrast. So Our Lord had instructed His followers to lay up treasure beyond the reach of rust or thief or subtle moth. "For where your treasure is there will your heart be also" (Luke 12:34). If we lose that high, exalted outlook, if we bend our eyes to the earth, our backs beneath its perishable burdens, our ideals to its low arc, then we forfeit our supernatural citizenship and run the risk of that terrible repudiation from the king: "I know you not" (Matt. 25:12).

Paul assured us: "you have come . . . to the city of the living God"; later on in the same letter, he warns us: "For we have not here a lasting city, but we seek one that is to come" (Heb. 12:22 and 13:14). As a result of baptism, "you are no more strangers and foreigners; but you are fellow citizens with the saints and the domestics of God" (Eph. 2:19). This week's liturgy, with its feast of all those saints already in possession of God and its commemoration of those whose consummation is delayed for a purgatorial interlude, drives home the point to us. We know what a naturalized citizen is; but we are supernaturalized citizens of the City of God, adopted sons of the Father, brothers to His Son, beloved of the Holy Spirit, destined for eternal happiness.

Yet we recklessly risk that priceless heritage for worldly success. Many a man worships "business enterprise" and its rewards; he holds that education should teach a young man how "to get on"; how his extravagance can keep pace with shrewd finance, how to be "self-satisfied . . . self-confident . . . money-getting"—while a far-off voice pronounces his doom: "Thou fool, this night do they require thy soul of thee: and whose shall those things be which thou hast provided?" (Luke 12:20). Only the fool makes a god of his belly, "minds the things of earth"; his ear attuned only to laughter and mad music cannot hear the Pauline plaint: "Their end is ruin."

Do All in the Name of the Lord

Colossians 3:17

That a man becomes what he thinks, that his ideals and the constant content of his mind shape and fashion him, is a psychological truism. So Edward Young, extolling a classical education, pointed out that its chief benefit for the young was contact with the greatest minds of all time. From that, by a "noble contagion," he contended, they would be inoculated with similar nobility.

Now the true Catholic is raised to a real though restricted share in the divine nature: "God became man," wrote Augustine, "in order that man might become God." It follows, then, that we should make God the primary tenant of our minds, the foremost object of our consciousness—an obligation, unfortunately, more often forgotten than fulfilled. If a man becomes what he thinks, and he keeps God constantly before him, the result is not hard to imagine; especially since God is quick and generous in giving that grace which will speed man's divinization.

This orienting of one's faculties toward God, the First Cause and Final End, should not be confined to times of formal prayer, be it vocal or mental, but should characterize all activities of life. It is this truth which Paul presents to us in the epistle of the Mass for the twenty-fourth Sunday after Pentecost: "All whatsoever you do in word or in work, do all in the name of the Lord Jesus Christ, giving thanks to God and to the Father by him." Then he lists some of those duties which can be transmuted into spiritual gold by the Midas touch of a right intention. Let wives be subject to their husbands, the latter solicitous for their wives, children obedient and docile, parents understanding towards their offspring.

The ordinary, monotonous work of life carried on in God, through God and for God can, therefore, emerge as the prayer of act. "Whatsoever you do, do it from the heart, as to the Lord, and not to men" (Col. 3:23). No action is too common or picayune to qualify, as Paul assures the Corinthians: "Therefore, whether you eat or drink, or whatsoever else you do, do all to the glory of God" (I Cor. 10:31).

Now that simple, supernatural fact can change your life profoundly, halo it with holiness, fire it to greatness. "If you eat, if you drink, if you marry, if you travel, do all in the name of God," says Chrysostom, "that is, calling Him to aid you . . . Do all in the name of the Lord, and He shall be prosperous to thee." If we dedicated each day to Him in sincere morning prayer, if we renewed that con-

secration with silent aspirations in subway, shop, office,
kitchen, factory; if we closed each day with another lifting
of our minds and hearts to Him, we should not long remain spiritually immature.

The traditional, heavily indulgenced manner of devot-
ing each day to Christ is the Morning Offering of the
Apostleship of Prayer. It hallows all the works, sufferings,
thoughts of one's day and, through Mary's Immaculate
Heart, offers them to the Sacred Heart. It unites the individual Catholic with his brethren throughout the world
in the blessed union of the Holy Sacrifice and common, in-
tegrated prayer; and it links each with Christ's Vicar on
earth.

Father Henry Ramière, tireless advocate of this apostolate
of prayer and its able theologian, was forever insisting on
the centrality of Christ in the real Catholic's thoughts and
life. "Jesus Christ," he says, "not only possesses the perfection of our nature; He also possesses the fulness of the
divinity . . . When God became man, He intended not
only to make man complete; most of all He had it in view
to make man divine . . . He is not only the model man,
but He is also the Head of humanity become divine."

There is our destiny—deification through Christ. Life
viewed that way becomes a lovely and adventurous affair
in which incidents painful, boring or inconsequential to
the children of this world become the raw material of glory
for the children of light. Whatever we do, with Him and
for Him, Christ dignifies and divinizes, but He requires
our conscious cooperation and love.

Made Worthy to Share the Lot of the Saints

Colossians 1:12

Liturgically, November is a month of reproach to the self-centered man, to him who has let his hat circumscribe his horizon. For it is a month of selflessness, of vast and long vistas. We have heard much in our time of global solidarity; we have watched various agencies at work to weld warring or wrangling nations into Mr. Willkie's "one world." But November reminds us Catholics of a unity which transcends time and space, of a truth which cements into community millions here on earth, in purgatory and in heaven; men of all races, colors, ages—the United Nations of the Communion of Saints.

Those who possess God in Heaven are not aloofly unmindful of us and our needs. Saint Jerome, consoling the widow Theodora, says of her husband: "He is enthroned in victory above, and beholds thee, and comforts thee in thy sorrow. He prepares for thee a place at his side." Chrysostom likewise assures a heartbroken widow that her loss is temporary and exhorts her to emulate the virtues of the husband she mourns: "Practise the virtues that he practised, and thou wilt be welcomed in the same abode where he now sits in glory, and wilt be united with him in the everlasting tabernacles."

It should be a great solace to us to reflect that those who have gone before us have not lost interest in us and that our eventual reunion with them will be chilled by no shadow of parting. Saint Bernard, disconsolate at the death of his brother Gerhard, comforted himself with that thought. Saint Anselm writes of the soul: "It loves its own friends even beyond the grave, and it will find them again and never lose them, if they are in God's presence." "Those who preceded us on our pilgrimage, and were not lost," says Saint Augustine, "will become the dearer to us the better we shall know them; and this love is free from all fear of separation."

But between us—the Church militant here on earth—and the Church triumphant in heaven, there is the purgatorial prison in which venial sins and the debt of punishment consequent on sin must be expiated. The suffering souls, our brethren also, cannot any longer merit for themselves, and they are dependent on our charity to shorten their term of suffering. Of them the sad proverb: "Out of sight, out of mind" is all too often verified. What comfort, what charity there is in the exhortation of Saint Ambrose: "We have loved them during life; let us not abandon them until we have conducted them by our prayers into the house of the Lord."

The Council of Trent solemnly assures us that the souls in purgatory "are helped by the suffrages of the faithful, and principally by the acceptable Sacrifice of the Altar." Augustine, long before, had told his people, the "prayers and alms of the faithful, the holy Sacrifice of the Altar aid the faithful departed and move the Lord to deal with them in mercy and kindness."

Sometimes we fall into the pagan idea of lavishing all our care on the grave of a dear departed or we exhaust our energies and express our sorrow in what the liturgy calls "fruitless and unavailing grief." It is well to treat the burial place of a departed soul with respect; it is proper and fitting to honor the vanishing remains of those who have gone before. Yet, "the dead," Chrysostom reminds us, "are not aided by tears but by prayer, intercession and alms." That is the invariable fact of Catholic dogmas; they are not merely glorious concepts to be admired, but operative truths from which grimly practical conclusions flow.

So with the Communion of Saints: it is a rebuke to pettiness, provincialism of mind, parochialism of heart. Under the headship of Christ, we are united with the angels and the blessed, with the suffering souls, with the millions of living Catholics who, in the conviction and grace of a common faith, still fight the good fight. On All Saints' Day we salute the victors and beg their intercession; on All Souls' Day we recall those who are saved but must be purified, and we intercede for them that God may shorten their suffering and bring them into full fruition. And in her exhortation over an open grave, the Church warns us to "bear in mind that we are most certainly to follow them."

Filled with Knowledge of God's Will

Colossians 1:9

Much of the mental dissonance, the spiritual static which hisses and crackles in our seething souls, comes from a deep rebelliousness which is as undogmatic as it is unhealthy. Reason and faith assure us that the God who made the world, and is omnipotently capable of running it, supervises still the affairs of men. He refuses to interfere with the liberty of His creatures but can, nevertheless, draw forth good even from their misdeeds. But all around us the feeling of rebellion, aggressive and articulate, encourages us to examine everything in the limited light and little logic of natural efficiency. Not even God is exempt from that arrogant examination; and since the infinite lies beyond man's mind, those who demand that everything be humanly analyzable, rebel; and their spirit can affect our own thinking.

Bit by bit we can be drawn toward the mentality described by Chrysostom: "Some persons . . . ask for an explanation of the judgments of God and strive to fathom that great deep." Rebuffed by the unfathomable, they become resentful; life, which, when viewed in the light of faith, is intelligible and exhilarating, becomes to them a jarring succession of frustrations and contradictions.

Against this sad outlook we find Paul writing in the epistle for the last Sunday after Pentecost. He assures the Colossians that he has been praying for them, "asking that you may be filled with knowledge of God's will, in all spiritual wisdom and understanding." May they, he adds, walking worthily of God and pleasing him, "be completely strengthened through his glorious power unto perfect patience and long-suffering."

There is the prescription for the person—and in these neurotic days his name is legion—whose lack of faith and vision has left him locked within himself, suffering from an ingrown and badly inflamed ego. Not only sanctity but, to a large degree, sanity and mental health depend upon our perception and acceptance of the divine design working out in our lives. It does not always unfold according to human blueprints; it may often seem flatly to reject them: "for the foolishness of God is wiser than men; and the weakness of God is stronger than men" (1 Cor. 1:25).

There is nothing fatalistic, quietistic or supine about this resignation, of course. In his brilliant book *This Tremendous Lover,* Father Boylan insists on the "positive and dynamic" nature of Christian spirituality. There is nothing neutral or negative about the building up of Christ within us. "And the whole scheme, as far as any one person in the state of grace is concerned, depends only on two wills; the will of God and his own will. It does not matter what other men will, what they do to him; if a man only cleave to God by his own will, God will sanctify him."

Christ's whole life was dominated by the will of the Father. "In the head of the book it is written of me: that I should do thy will, O God" (Heb. 10:7); His first recorded utterance dedicated Him primarily to "His Father's business" (Luke 2:49). During His hidden years He was subject to those who were the authoritative channels of that will (Luke 2:51); in His public life His meat was the same holy will (John 4:34): He taught us to pray "Thy will be done" (Matt. 6:10); in His agony He exemplified that prayer (Mark 14:36); He died with a final, filial salute to His Father (Luke 23:46). That was the way of the Christ; there is no other way for the Christian.

The time comes when, as C. S. Lewis said, a man bows and says to God "Thy will be done," or when God, refusing to limit man's liberty, yields to his perversity and says to him "*thy* will be done." That first submission means happiness here, heaven hereafter; that second inversion of proper order spells horror now and hell forever. And "in His will is our peace" is one of Dante's best loved lines. To seek peace elsewhere is foolish, futile, dogmatically fatal.

Key to Christian Humanism

One chill night in November, 1848, a closed carriage raced
out of Rome and swung up towards the town of Gaeta,
over the Neopolitan border. Huddled in its swaying seat
sat Pope Pius IX.

Loud above the horses' hooves, the clatter of the out-
riders and the frantic wheels, rose the clamor in the city
behind. Rome was in revolt: the gallant Swiss Guards had
been forced to capitulate and disband. Count Rossi, the
papal Prime Minister, lay dead beneath the assassin's
stiletto; it was the day of Cavour, Gioberti, Victor Emman-
uel and a camarilla of secret societies whose common
deadly enemy was the Pope. *Il dolce Christo in terra*, as
Catherine of Siena was wont to call the Holy Father in

another day of anti-papal upheaval, was fleeing for his life.

Axiomatic in Catholic thought is the principle "Where Peter is, there is the Church." Gradually the papal court formed itself again at Gaeta and, in exile, Peter's successor continued Peter's work.

Pius had for a long time desired to canonize the universal Catholic belief in Mary's Immaculate Conception, with a solemn definition, an authoritative declaration that it was God's revelation.

From Gaeta he consulted by letter 603 bishops of the Church, asking for their opinion. Of these, 546 held that the Immaculate Conception was a revealed truth; some few suspended judgment; about twelve disliked the proposed definition because it would stigmatize as heretics those who denied the doctrine; only five were unqualifiedly opposed. Twenty-four Bishops, while they held that the Immaculate Conception was revealed truth, thought a definition at that time would be inopportune.

The Gaeta exile ended and, back in Rome, five years later, on December 8, 1854, Pius promulgated his decree. It was a brilliant occasion. With almost two hundred bishops and a vast crowd of the faithful present, the Pontiff celebrated High Mass. Thousands of voices took up the ancient invocation to the Holy Spirit and Pius spoke the solemn words:

We declare, pronounce, and define that the doctrine which holds that the Blessed Virgin Mary, at the first instant of her conception, by a singular privilege and grace of the Omnipotent God, in virtue of the merits of Jesus Christ, the Saviour of mankind, was preserved immaculate from all stain of original sin, has been revealed by God, and therefore should firmly and constantly be believed by all the faithful.

The Pontiff's voice faltered, his eyes filled, he intoned the *Te Deum* and 50,000 voices took it up. Outside, the cannon of Castel San Angelo roared, the bells of 300 churches thrilled Rome; and from steeple to steeple across Italy and Europe, the joyous tidings rang.

Time has shown the opportuneness of the definition. For Pius' age, as one Catholic scholar has pointed out, still clove to the "old Rousseauian heresy of man's natural perfection," apotheosizing human nature and shrugging off sin. Naturalism, liberalism, rationalism and the very rebelliousness which had driven Pius to Gaeta that dark night, were aflame all over Europe.

Now Pius' definition was an impressive reminder to man that sin was his common, inescapable heritage; that Rousseau was wrong, that Saint Paul, Catholic tradition and the Councils of Orange and Trent gave man's real biography. Only by a singular privilege, and in the antici- pated light of her divine Son's merits, was Christ's own Mother preserved from this universal doom.

Though it was, in one sense, an implicit rebuke to man, the declaration of the Immaculate Conception was defi- nitely an assurance as well. Then as now, men were struggling for freedom, for liberation. They felt the es- sential "antagonism at the heart of things," and no phil- osophical return to the "noble savage" or to the fiction of a "Golden Age" could help them blink the bleak facts of everyday life. They were lost in a world they could not understand, a world which was to them, as to Matthew Arnold, "a brazen prison." There was a speculative opti- mism abroad, but with it went a widespread, practical des- pair. Kant had virtually incarcerated man within his own soul and succeeding thinkers had only tightened the bolts.

Philosophy and religion, outside of the Catholic Church, were suffering from a severe dislocation of man's ego, accompanied by a pronounced swelling.

Into this intellectual, political and social restlessness, the definition of the Immaculate Conception came as a reconciliation of man's fears with his hopes. It showed him the cause of the surging forces of evil within him and the downward drag toward despair. It explained to him again that his heritage was soiled, his ancestry tainted.

Adam, whom God appointed head of the human race, proved also to be the father of anthropocentric humanism. He disobeyed the divine prohibition and infected human nature with original sin. It is this diseased human nature which comes down by natural generation to all of Adam's posterity. Because of that sin man has gross inclinations, fifth columnists within his own gates, to cooperate with Satan, the enemy beseiging him from without.

All men, the doctrine of the Immaculate Conception explains, are subject to this law of inherited sin by the very fact that they derive naturally from Adam. And the unique remedy is the redemptive grace which Christ merited by His Passion and death.

It is that grace which liberates men from the bondage of sin: it was likewise that grace which preserved Mary, Christ's Mother, from the actual contamination to which, as a daughter of Adam and Eve, she would otherwise have been liable. Our redemption is liberative: hers was preservative.

That was the truth which Pius IX, on December 8, 1854, declared to be revealed by God and firmly to be believed by all the faithful. Never, for one single instant, was Mary befouled with the contagion of sin. From the

first second of the union of her body and soul in the womb
of her mother, Saint Ann, she was completely spotless.
She, too, was redeemed by her divine Son. For her, in
fact, He was pre-eminently a Redeemer because, as Ulla-
thorne points out, it is greater to protect one from con-
tracting a debt than to dissolve the debt after one has
contracted it.

That, in simplest terms, is what we mean by the Immaculate Conception. It is often misunderstood, as Newman, writing to Pusey, lamented:

> It is to me a strange phenomenon, that so many learned and
> devout men stumble at this doctrine; and I can only account
> for it by supposing that in matter of fact they do not know
> what we mean by the Immaculate Conception.

But the foregoing summary of the doctrine is only a
brief sketch according to its historical and theological
scope. Viewed even thus starkly, it unriddles many of the
mysteries which still confuse the sages in the days of Pius
XII no less than in the time of Pius IX.

Man realizes that he is neither wholly good nor completely bad. He finds within himself soaring aspirations
which make him kin to the angels, and co-existent with
them a gravitational pull down toward brotherhood with
the apes. Understood in its full background, the Immaculate Conception rationalizes these conflicting inclinations
and points out the way of reconciling them.

It justifies man's hope, because it shows him the heights
to which one human being, a modest Jewish girl, was
elevated. And it sternly insists that her elevation was
achieved not through science, philosophy, art, nor the
evolutionary ripening of man to supernature, but by the
power of God.

Yet, by reminding man that Mary alone escaped the wound and scar of original sin, the doctrine also explains man's evil inclinations. He is weak and the forces of evil are strong; of himself he has not the power to walk in self-sufficient arrogance, but must proceed warily, in fear and trembling. Only the grace of Christ, which preserved Mary from sin, can release man and enable him to fulfill his destiny and press on to that far country where at last he will feel no more the vague, nostalgic ache which had vexed his soul for so long.

These were the related truths which Pius IX recalled to restless Europe in 1854. His definition capped four centuries of solid tradition and came as no innovation or shock to Catholic consciousness, which had assented from earliest times. From 1476 to 1708, nineteen of Pius' predecessors, with varying degrees of directness and force, had approved the doctrine, and the Council of Trent had acknowledged it. The great religious orders, with one exception, had taught and preached it for years. About the time that young John Berchmans was making a vow, which he signed in his blood, to propound and defend the truth of the Immaculate Conception, there were 150 universities professing it in Europe, England and America.

Mary, the Immaculate Mother, had always been an ideal with an immeasurable impact on European civilization. She was no pale, poetic Beatrice, no purple and hazy Guinevere, but a flesh-and-blood woman, in whose virginal womb the Word was made flesh. Born in Palestine, she transcended all nationality and belonged to all nations. For centuries, in Christian Europe, devotion to the Madonna gave, in John Ruskin's phrase, "sanctity to the humblest duties and comfort to the sorest trials of the lives of women." Lecky, in his *History of European Morals,* speaking of the "Catholic reverence for the Virgin," declares:

> It has had an influence which the worship of the pagan goddesses could never possess, for these had been almost destitute of moral beauty, and especially of that kind of moral beauty which is peculiarly feminine. It supplied in a great measure the redeeming and ennobling element in that strange amalgam of religious, licentious and military feeling which was formed around women in the age of chivalry, and which no succeeding change of habit or belief has wholly destroyed.

That influence received new impetus from the definition of the Immaculate Conception; and a few years later, Bernadette was to call the whole world to Lourdes to express its devotion to Mary.

Now, as then, we live in a restless world peopled by men who cannot understand it or themselves. The message of the mystery and the feast of the Immaculate Conception is obvious. For us as Americans, it should have special significance. By decree of the Baltimore Council, Mary in her Immaculate Conception is the patroness of the United States; during the war she was patroness also of the Military Ordinariate. But devotion to her in this hemisphere is no new growth. Before the Pilgrim fathers landed, the Universities of Lima and Mexico, following the lead of their European peers, had bound their members by vow to assert and defend the truth of the Immaculate Conception.

The Concept of Christian Patriotism

Prejudice is a sorry handmaid for either philosophy or philology. One need but think of the eighteenth-century usage of the adjective "Gothic"—which we associate reverently with Chartres—to designate Horace Walpole's *Castle of Otranto*. In the course of that same brilliant and brittle age, another word, "patriot," fell into disrepute and became, as Macaulay notes, "a byword of derision." It was used, Dr. Johnson declared, "ironically for a fractious disturber of the government." Knowing that, we feel less resentful at Dryden's apparently cynical line, "Never was patriot yet, but was a fool," or at Pope's wry generalization, "A patriot is a fool in every age."

Cicero had said some glowing things about love of country and Horace's *Dulce et decorum est pro patria mori* is one of those epigrams which every school boy allegedly knows. Nonetheless, the idea of patriotism, as we know it, is relatively modern. During the one hundred and fifty years before Dryden and Pope the word was in good standing. But then hysterical partisanship arrogated the predicate "patriotic" to itself and vitiated both term and idea. This was the background of the remark attributed to Dr. Johnson that patriotism was the last refuge of a scoundrel.

At the moment, "patriotism" is the word on everyone's lips, the idea in everyone's mind. At the moment, likewise, post-bellum passion and prejudice are bubbling fiercely and well might corrode once more the validity of a splendid idea and ideal. There is need for clear thought in the matter not only in the interests of pure speech but accurate appreciation and intelligent action as well. We have had trenchant articles on the terrible acid of hate which can eat away not only words and ideas but human hearts and minds. We have tried after this last war not to permit hysteria and demagoguery to forge war anew at the peace councils as they had after the first world war. But there are many false ideas abroad about man's relations to the state, about man's primary loyalties, ideas which are really burlesques and parodies of real patriotism.

For real patriotism is a Christian virtue. It cannot therefore include, as an essential component, vicious hatred; it cannot be founded on lies; it cannot condone wrong nor, under some phrase like "the exigencies of national security," make immorality permissible. Stephen Decatur, a gallant American, spoke a stirring toast to his "country right or wrong." Far better than a reasoned refutation of the attitude was Chesterton's devastating comment: "It is like saying 'My mother, drunk or sober.'"

In reducing Decatur to absurdity, Chesterton does well to hint a parallel between the attitude a man should have toward his mother and the regard he should have for his country. For Saint Thomas taught that because our parents and our country gave us birth and nourishment, "consequently man is debtor chiefly to his parents and his country, after God."

Man is, by his very nature, social. History attests this, the Church teaches it; nor have the sophistries of Hobbes and Rousseau ever obscured the fact. Men have always lived in groups, and part of the social bond which solidified those units of mutually dependent men has always been the loyalty with which God endowed human nature. Involuntarily and under dictate of the natural law, we feel affection for our place of birth and growth, for the dear persons of our family and our friends, for the ideas and backgrounds against which we lived and moved. The "country" which is the object of our love and patriotism is, then, not only a particular region of earth into which the ashes of our ancestors have long since fused. It includes also persons, ideas, traditions.

To this mandate of the natural law, inclining man to filial affection for the place of his birth, Pope Leo XIII has given eloquent testimony:

> The natural law enjoins us to love devotedly and to defend the country in which we had birth and in which we were reared, so that every good citizen hesitates not to face death for his native land.

Pius XI likewise acclaims patriotism as the motive force of high virtue and heroism; and he makes it clear that he is speaking of a patriotism which is "kept within the bounds of the law of Christ."

That qualification, of course, is merely corollary to the fundamental principle in this whole matter, laid down centuries ago by Eternal Wisdom: "Render unto Caesar the things that are Caesar's, and to God the things that are God's." The only peril, therefore, in a Christian and virtuous love of country is the same danger latent in the love of any other creature—excess. As Pius XI points out, "true love of country" can be "debased to the condition of an extreme nationalism," an apotheosis of one's own land, language, compatriots and traditions, and can have, as its malicious correlative, contempt for all others. Recent history has given us examples of that truth. "Patriotism," Chesterton once wrote, "is not the first virtue. Patriotism rots into Prussianism when you pretend it is the first virtue."

In the Middle Ages, there was a transcendental "nationality" which the whole Christian commonwealth acknowledged. For the common *patria* towards which all were striving, in relation to which all were *viatores,* was heaven. Here on earth the Church, the "City of God," drew her citizens from all localities and overshadowed their Pentecostal multiplicity of tongues with the unifying roof of a common ideal. Hence, while a Christian man was attached to his own region, his own "nation," his Christianity and his constant conviction that we have not here a lasting city, kept his nationalism from becoming extreme or supreme.

Modern times, however, emphasized nationality and the lines of language which separate men, so that the Pentecostal unity was ruptured and Babel rebuilt. The breakdown of the old concept of world citizenship and the emergence of distinct nationalities had many causes.

Easily chief of these was the jettisoning of supernatural and supranational religion which had been the real cement of the medieval social structure. Once men forgot their common brotherhood and the all-inclusive fatherhood of God, the individual assumed a new and compensatory importance he had not known before. The state became the necessary regulator of individualism run riot, and, bit by bit, the state loomed larger in the scheme of things. Nationality had come to stay.

Nationality is primarily cultural and not, as it is often supposed, racial. The racial approach will help us scarcely at all in arriving at any clear notion of nationality. For, in the last analysis, nationality stems from a difference in language, a divergence of historical tradition and culture. The French, the English and the Germans, for example, are separate nationalities; each group has evolved by processes indigenous to its own country, climate and racial genius; each has its own literature, each treasures its own deposit of tradition. The Church has always acknowledged and encouraged nationalities. Recall how mightily she contributed towards the retention of a national consciousness in such countries as Ireland and Poland when they had no political independence. So she would never object to what Pius XI calls "lawful love of country and a sentiment of *justifiable* nationalism."

The true Christian nationalism, then, conforms to the law of Christ. It does not swell into jingoistic, international browbeating, nor chauvinism; nor, if it be circumscribed by that law of Christ, does it condescend to "lesser breeds without the law." It cannot permit the state to become the ultimate focus of man's loyalty; for it knows that the state is not an end, but a means to an end. True Christian nationalism wears that badge and banner which Christ designated as the mark of those who really follow Him—charity. It is incumbent on the Christian state as on the Christian individual to reconcile the natural, God-given love of one's own land and region and tongue with the international and supranational command: "Love thy neighbor." "The gospel," wrote Benedict XV, "does not contain one law of charity for individuals, and another law, different from the first, for cities and peoples."

Contrast with that serene sanity an example of the deification of the state which, in our sad day, caused so much grief to the world:

> The concept of race and people has now been raised to that sacred level and forms our law for the present and the future . . . Our future depends only on ourselves, not on Rome or Judea . . . There will be neither dogma nor Church, only the German community. No confession, not even a general Christian Church, but only one people that believes in God and in itself!

To such lengths of what one might call national narcissism can a race go, once it exiles Christ and His Church.

First-born of this "hard egotistical nationalism," as Pius XI calls it, is intolerance. The terrible persecutions which have been directed against Jews and Catholics, in our memory, can be laid at the door of nationalism. And even within our own free and enlightened land, at certain bleak periods of history, this particular form of fanaticism, which dimensionalized itself here as "nativism," has generated such monstrosities as the Ku Klux Klan. And there are not wanting general indications even now, that men who prize religious liberty must keep guard against what, with a bow to Thomas Hardy, we might call "the return of the nativist."

Any race infected by febrile nationalism must inevitably come to look on Christ's law of charity as a soft and decadent shibboleth. Convinced of its own superiority and its destiny to dominate other nations, it must necessarily bend all of its forces and corporate energies to militarism. It must indoctrinate its young men with the creed of fang and claw, harden its adolescents to replace their elders in the ranks, and suckle its infants on a spear. It must teach its people's pulses to dance to the tempo of the drumbeat, to race with fever at the sight of a flag. It has to "let the family home, and with it the school, become merely an anteroom to the battlefields," as Pope Pius XII warned. Only with contempt, can it hear his calm voice call for "an honest peace of justice and moderation." It cannot brook any restriction on a man's devotion to his country, even if that restriction be divine.

It is good, then, at a time like this to pause and think out the true meaning of patriotism. For the law of Christ, far from depriving a man of his patriotism, rather canonizes it for him, gives it a new glow and glory, makes it a derivative, as Aquinas teaches, of the Fourth Commandment. It is no longer a temporary inner flash of sentiment, aroused by oratory and whipped up by propaganda, but a virtue lineally related to the filial devotion with which a man loves his father and mother.

Such patriotism can make of the intelligent Catholic a good citizen and, if need be, an unflinching soldier; for it requires him to base his service, civilian or military, on the high and holy ground of duty to God. How much

better and less likely to crumble is courage which results
from conviction illumined by grace rather than from the
slogan-thinking of a time of crisis.

In our present, uneasy age, then, we would do well to
ponder the true concept of patriotism. For it will help us
through the steel-gray days ahead. More important still,
it will teach us the real relationships which must govern
any lasting internationalism—justice, charity, the brotherhood of man and the fatherhood of God. And unless those
considerations prevail at our peace tables, any armistice
will last long enough only for exhausted and embittered
belligerent nations to recover and rearm.

READINGS

Readings

Some Selected Readings Suitable to Arouse
an Interest in Saint Paul and an
Understanding of His Epistles

Bover, M., *Three Studies from St. Paul*, London, 1931
Boylan, P., St. *Paul's Epistle to the Romans*, Dublin, 1934
Callan, C. J., *The Epistles of St. Paul*, New York, 1931, 2
    volumes
Catholic Biblical Association of America, *A Commentary on
    the New Testament*, New York, 1942
Cerny, E., *Firstborn of Every Creature* (Col. 1, 15) Baltimore,
    1938
Coghlan, P., St. *Paul: His Life, Work and Spirit*, London, 1920
Eaton, R., *Epistles of St. Paul to the Thessalonians*, London,
    1939
—— St. *Paul's Epistles to the Colossians and Philemon with
    Introduction and Notes*, London, 1934.

Fouard, C., *St. Paul and His Missions,* New York, 1915
   The Last Years of St. Paul, New York, 1915
Herbst, Winfrid, *The Epistles as I know Them,* New York,
   1947
Heuser, H., *From Tarsus to Rome,* New York, 1929
Hitchcock, G., *Epistle to the Ephesians,* New York, 1913
Holzner, J., *Paul of Tarsus,* St. Louis, 1944
—— *à Lapide, Cornelius, Commentary of First Corinthians,*
   London, 1896 (Hodges)
Lattey, C. F., and Others, *St. Paul and His Teaching,* London,
   1930
—— *Paul,* Milwaukee, 1939
—— *Readings in First Corinthians, Church Beginnings in
   Greece,* St. Louis, 1928
MacEvilly, *An Exposition of the Epistles of St. Paul and of the
   Catholic Epistles,* Dublin, 1875
MacRory, J. *Epistles of St. Paul to the Corinthians,* Dublin,
   1935
Maritain, J., *The Living Thoughts of St. Paul,* New York, 1941
Martindale, C. C., *St. Paul,* London, 1924
—— *Princes of His People: II St. Paul,* New York, 1925
McGarry, W., *Paul and the Crucified,* New York, 1939
Monro, M. T., *Enjoying the New Testament,* New York, 1945
Parker, M., *Introduction to the Acts of the Apostles and the
   Epistles of St. Paul,* New York, 1927
Pieper, K., *St. Paul,* New York, 1928
Prat, F., *The Theology of St. Paul,* New York, 1927, 2 volumes
—— *St. Paul,* New York, 1928
Ryan, C., *The Epistles of the Sundays and Festivals,* Dublin,
   1931, 2 volumes
Tricot, A. E., *St. Paul: the Apostle of the Gentiles,* St. Louis,
   1930

Additional Readings

Bandas, R., *Biblical Questions: New Testament,* Paterson, 1936
—— *Master Idea of St. Paul's Epistles on the Redemption,*
   Brudges, 1925

Chleyer, L. J., *The Pauline Formula 'Induere Christum' with Special reference to the Works of St. John Chrysostom*, Washington, 1921

Cohausz, O., *The Priest and St. Paul*, New York, 1927

Dupperay, *Christ in Christian Life According to St. Paul*, New York, 1927

Giordani, I., *St. Paul, Apostle and Martyr*, New York, 1946

Jacquier, E., *History of the Books of the New Testament*, Vol. I: "St. Paul and His Epistles," London, 1907

Piconio, B., *Exposition of the Epistles of St. Paul*, London, 1888

Pope, H., *The Catholic Student's 'Aids' to the Bible*, London, 1938 (2nd ed.,) 5 volumes

Rickaby, J., *Notes on St. Paul: Corinthians, Galatians, Romans*, New York, 1905

—— *Further Notes on St. Paul: The Epistles of the Captivity*, London, 1911

Steinmueller, J., *A Companion to Scripture Studies* (Vol. III. Special introduction to the New Testament) New York, 1943

Steinmueller, J., and Sullivan, K., *A Companion to the New Testament*, New York, 1943

Westminster Version of the Sacred Scriptures, Vols. 3 and 4. London

Wilberforce, B., *Devout Commentary on the Epistles to the Ephesians*, St. Louis, 1902